PRAYING THROUGH THE
100
GATEWAY CITIES
OF THE 10/40 WINDOW

SECOND EDITION

Edited by C. Peter Wagner, Stephen Peters & Mark Wilson

YWAM Publishing
Seattle, Washington

YWAM Publishing is the publishing ministry of Youth With A Mission (YWAM), an international missionary organization of Christians from many denominations dedicated to presenting Jesus Christ to this generation. To this end, YWAM has focused its efforts in three main areas: (1) training and equipping believers for their part in fulfilling the Great Commission (Matthew 28:19), (2) personal evangelism, and (3) mercy ministry (medical and relief work).

For a free catalog of books and materials, call (425) 771-1153 or (800) 922-2143. Visit us online at www.ywampublishing.com.

Praying through the 100 Gateway Cities of the 10/40 Window
Copyright © 1995, 2010 by YWAM Publishing
Second Edition

Published by YWAM Publishing
a ministry of Youth With A Mission
P.O. Box 55787, Seattle, WA 98155

Grateful acknowledgment is made for permission to adapt and reprint the following articles:
   "What Is the 10/40 Window?" Joshua Project, www.joshuaproject.net/10-40 -window.php. Parts of this article were adapted from Luis Bush, "Explaining the 10/40 Window," in *The Great Commission Handbook* (Evanston, Ill.: Berry Publishing, 1994).
   Viv Grigg, "Intercessors and Cosmic Urban Spiritual Warfare," *International Journal of Frontier Missions* 10, no. 4 (1993).
   Fred Markert, "11,000 Reasons Why Jesus Won't Come Back Yet," *The Last Days Magazine* 16, no. 2 (1993).

Scripture quotations in this book are taken from the Holy Bible, New International Version. Copyright © 1973, 1978, 1984 by International Bible Society. Used by permission of Zondervan. All rights reserved.

Cover illustrations by Julie Bosacker. Used by permission.

ISBN 978-1-57658-522-1

Second printing 2012

Printed in the United States of America

To the believers and workers
in the 100 Gateway Cities

CONTENTS

CENTRAL ASIA   77

INTRODUCTION

*What other nation is so great as to have their gods near them the
way the Lord our God is near us whenever we pray to him?*
—Deuteronomy 4:7

*But you are a chosen people, a royal priesthood, a holy nation, a
people belonging to God, that you may declare the praises of him
who called you out of darkness into his wonderful light.*
—1 Peter 2:9

Christians have the amazing privilege to pray to the one true
God, who is near them and hears their requests. This book,
which first came into existence in 1995, has been a guide for over
36 million people (that is not a misprint) to pray for the "gateway
cities" of the 10/40 Window. In addition, some 10,000 prayer jour-
neyers went into these cities to pray on site. All this took place as
part of Praying Through the Window II, a global prayer initiative
led by AD2000 & Beyond.

That is not all. In 1997, Praying Through the Window III
expanded the global prayer initiative to pray for unreached people in the 10/40 Window. Upwards of 50 million people joined

in intercession, and again thousands of people traveled to pray on site. In 1999, Praying Through the Window IV continued the global initiative, focusing its efforts in new and strategic ways by praying for Million People Target Areas (MPTAs), as researched by Campus Crusade for Christ. Many ministries, such as the Joshua Project, have carried on the work begun in the twentieth century into the twenty-first century.

Books, papers, and other resources have played a key role in uniting Christians for this global task of praying for the nations and fulfilling the Great Commission. Many books have served for a time, and some have been revised multiple times to unite praying Christians worldwide. *Praying Through the 100 Gateway Cities of the 10/40 Window* has continued to be used by many people, and the time came to update some of its information so that Christians remain as informed — and our prayers remain as effective — as possible.

A major reason that this book continues to be relevant is its focus on cities. The migration of thousands upon thousands of people from rural areas to urban areas has not decreased but increased in the last decade. In fact, urbanization is a growing global phenomenon. The UN has reported that the global proportion of urban population increased from 29 percent in 1950 to 50 percent in 2010. The UN projects that 60 percent of the world's population will live in cities by 2030. It is no wonder that the population of the majority of the cities in this book has grown substantially since the book was first published. As a result, the importance of these cities in spreading the good news about Jesus throughout the world is greater now than ever before.

The information in this revised edition has been updated based on the most recent and reliable sources available to the best of our knowledge. However, statistical information is provided primarily as a means of comparison and as an aid to pray, and should not be regarded as authoritative.

WHY PRAY?

Michael Little
President, Christian Broadcasting Network

In the midst of today's fast-paced and high-tech lifestyle, what a privilege it is to unite in prayer for one hundred of the least evangelized cities! But what is God's heart for the residents who are among the neediest, spiritually and materially, in the world? Most relevant for our day is 2 Peter chapter 3, where God reveals his heart and points to where our hearts should be as committed believers in the Lord Jesus Christ.

Peter's emphasis on the fact of Jesus' return, and how we should then live and think, separates the popular "live for now" temporal values from those that are eternal. Moreover, contemporary Bible translations use a phrase repeated three times in verses 12, 13, and 14 — "looking forward" — which speaks of the day Jesus will return and when we, his followers, will be with him.

Peter says that this attitude of increasing expectation should result in a more disciplined spiritual life. But, very significantly, he says in verse 12 that we can actually hasten or "speed its coming," referring to the day of Christ's return.

This is an awesome concept and responsibility, that we could so dramatically influence such an event by our attitudes and actions. But it is consistent with Matthew 24:14, where Jesus says his return is contingent on the fulfillment of the Great Commission: "And this gospel of the kingdom will be preached in the whole world as a testimony to all nations, and then the end will come."

The monumental task of motivating the church to fulfill the Great Commission can be overwhelming. However, Jesus taught us that he is the burden bearer. It is our duty and privilege to pray and to discuss these overwhelming responsibilities with him. Yet we are to be specific in our prayers.

- We are to pray for the harvest workers (Matthew 9:36–38).
- We are to pray for the needed changes in ourselves that he wants to accomplish for his purposes (2 Peter 3:14–18).
- We are to pray that we will see the world with God's love and compassion, as did Christian statesman Bob Pierce, who prayed "to have our hearts broken with the things that break the heart of God."

From a human view, reaching the world through our current physical means is possible. The technology exists to penetrate every geographic and political barrier. Shortwave radio has reached around the globe for decades. Satellite delivery of TV signals is now worldwide. CNN television news demonstrates global saturation by being available on satellite over every country on the earth.

But ours is a spiritual battle for which prayer is the only answer! We need focus in our spiritual goals. This guide will assist you in praying through the 100 Gateway Cities. Thank you for joining us, whether at home or on site, as we pray for God's kingdom to come and his will to be done among the unreached peoples in these strategic cities.

WHAT IS THE
10/40 WINDOW?

The core of the unreached people of our world lives in a rectangular-shaped window. It is a belt that extends from West Africa across Asia between 10 and 40 degrees north of the equator. If we are serious about providing a valid opportunity for every people and city to experience the love, truth, and saving power of Jesus Christ, we cannot ignore the reality that we must concentrate on this region of the world termed "the 10/40 Window."

Historical Significance

Why do committed Christians need to focus on the 10/40 Window? The first reason is because of the historical and biblical significance of this part of the world. It is in the 10/40 Window that we encounter the account of Adam and Eve in the Garden of Eden. Man was to keep, or guard, God's paradise and have dominion over the earth and subdue it; however, Adam and Eve failed to guard God's paradise and forfeited the right to rule over the earth. Then came the flood, followed by the building of the tower of Babel. This effort by man to rally together in defiance of God resulted in the introduction of different languages, the scattering of the people, and the formation of nations. After this, ancient history played out in the territory marked by the 10/40 Window, from the cradle of civilization in Mesopotamia across the Fertile Crescent to Egypt. Ancient empires came and went. The fate of God's people Israel rose and fell depending on their obedience to the covenant with their God. Here Christ was born, lived his life, died on the cross, and rose again.

It was not until the second missionary journey of the apostle Paul, toward the end of the biblical record, that events of divine history occurred outside of the territory identified as the 10/40 Window. For the committed Christian, the fact that so much of God's dealing with humanity took place on the piece of earth encompassed by the 10/40 Window is a significant reason to focus on it.

Unevangelized Peoples

There is a second reason why committed Christians should focus on the 10/40 Window. While this is only one-third of the earth's total land area, almost two-thirds of the people in the world reside here. Moreover, 78 percent of all unreached people groups live in the 10/40 Window. We need to think of the mission of Christ, who came to seek and to save the lost, as taught in the parables about the lost sheep and the lost coin. Christ made great efforts to heal, restore, and save every person. When we consider Christ's mandate to preach the gospel to everyone, to make disciples of all the nations, and to be his witnesses to the uttermost parts of the earth, it becomes clear that we must focus our efforts on the 10/40 Window.

Three Religious Blocs

A third reason to focus on the 10/40 Window is that it is where three main religious blocs are located. There is the Muslim bloc stretching across North Africa and the Middle East. There is the Hindu bloc centered in South Asia. And there is the Buddhist bloc in Southeast Asia. In addition to these three religious blocs, China constitutes a significant nonreligious portion of the world.

The Poor

The fourth reason to focus our attention on the 10/40 Window is that the poor are there. In fact, more than eight out of ten of the poorest of the poor, who on average live on less than $500 per person per year, live in the 10/40 Window. Despite the fact that the majority of the poor and the unreached live in the 10/40 Window, only 8 percent of all missionaries work among these people. Bryant Myers of World Vision has suggested that "the poor are lost, and the lost are poor." There is a remarkable overlap between the poorest countries of the world and the least evangelized countries of the world. This certainly constitutes one of the greatest challenges of our time.

Quality of Life

A fifth reason to focus on the 10/40 Window is related to the quality of life. One way of measuring the quality of life has been to combine three variables: life expectancy, infant mortality, and literacy. More than eight out of ten of the people living in the fifty countries of the world with the lowest quality of life also live in the 10/40 Window. This represents 47 percent of the population, yet only 8 percent of the foreign missionary force works among these people. Over nine out of ten of these people live in Hindu or Muslim countries.

The psalmist wrote, "Blessed is the nation whose God is the LORD" (Psalm 33:12). Certainly, in comparing the relationship of the quality of life in the 10/40 Window with that in those countries which have a higher percentage of Christians, it becomes apparent that the Lord God blesses a nation that turns to him. Yet, in turn, he expects the nation who is blessed to be a blessing to other nations, as it says in Psalm 67:1–2: "May God be gracious to us and bless us and make his face shine upon us, that your ways may be known on earth, your salvation among all nations."

Stronghold of Satan

Why do committed Christians need to focus on the 10/40 Window? Because it is a stronghold of Satan. The people living in the 10/40 Window have suffered not only hunger and a lower quality of life compared with the rest of humanity, but have also been kept from the transforming, life-giving, community-changing power of the gospel.

The Scripture makes it clear from the writings of Paul the apostle that "the god of this age has blinded the minds of unbelievers, so that they cannot see the light of the gospel of the glory of Christ, who is the image of God" (2 Corinthians 4:4).

In the same letter, the apostle writes in 10:3–4, "For though we live in the world, we do not wage war as the world does. The weapons we fight with are not the weapons of the world. On the contrary, they have divine power to demolish strongholds." It appears from a careful observation of the 10/40 Window that Satan has established a territorial stronghold with his forces to restrain the advance of the gospel in that territory.

We need to significantly increase our efforts to reach those who are in the 10/40 Window. If we are to be faithful to Scripture and obedient to the mandate of Christ, if we are to see the establishment of a mission-minded church-planting movement within every unreached people and city, if we are to give all peoples a valid opportunity to experience the love, truth, and saving power of Jesus Christ, we must get down to the core of the unreached — the 10/40 Window.

THE CHALLENGE OF THE
10/40 WINDOW

Fred Markert

Director, YWAM Network for Strategic Initiatives

Almost every time the Bible mentions the word *nations,* it refers not to political countries like France, India, or Australia but to people groups. Biblical nations are people groups, such as the Berber in Morocco, the Kurds in Iraq, the Navajo in America, or the Pitjanjara in Australia. It is calculated that there are about 24,000 distinct ethnic groups in the world today. A people group is defined as any grouping that has specific characteristics such as geographic location, language, religion, or culture.

We have reached 13,000 of these groups with the gospel, but 11,000 still have not heard. In Matthew 24:14 Jesus told us that the end would not come until all peoples have had an opportunity to hear the gospel.

A Promise of Blessing

God's goal from the beginning of time was for humanity to fill the earth and rule it while enjoying intimate relationship with him. This ideal situation was shattered when sin entered the world, turning our perfect planet into a raging war zone. Though man purposely turned his back on God, the loving Creator still desired

19

relationship with his creation. All of history is the account of his plan to bring that about — and the story begins with one man.

When God began looking for someone whose heart was open to him, he was impressed with Abraham. In Genesis 12:2–3 God promises to Abraham, "I will make you into a great nation . . . and all the peoples on earth will be blessed through you." This promise is reaffirmed to both Abraham and Isaac (Genesis 22:18; 26:4), with God making a solemn covenant with Abraham that "through your offspring all nations on earth will be blessed." This blessing was ultimately fulfilled through Jesus, who came to reconcile all people to God. Jesus was sent to ensure that all peoples would know him.

The 10/40 Window

Seventy-eight percent of all unreached people groups and some 80 percent of the world's poor, as well as most of the world's Muslims, Hindus, and Buddhists, live in the 10/40 Window.

These groups are not masses of faceless people but individuals whom God loves intimately. He knows the Puku-Geeri-Keri-Wipsi of Nigeria, the Bozos of Mali, the Hwla of Togo, and the Thae of Laos. He does not want any of them to perish, but all to come to repentance (2 Peter 3:9).

Tragically, most of these people groups have absolutely no access to the gospel. They have no Bible, no Christian literature, no radio or television programs. There is no one to tell them. They will never come to the Lord if no one takes the gospel to them. Yes, we have needs at home, but the only way the Puku-Geeri-Keri-Wipsi will ever hear is if Christians leave home to reach them.

World Evangelization

The world can be divided into three population segments:

- *Christian world.* That part which has heard the gospel and been influenced greatly by it.
- *Evangelized non-Christian world.* That part in which up to 50 percent of the people have been evangelized but are still resistant.

- **Unevangelized world.** That part which has never heard the gospel and is often removed geographically, culturally, and linguistically from Christianity.

A pastor once asked me, "Why should we dedicate money, people, and prayer to reach the Muslims over in Africa and the Middle East when my city is so needy and so many here don't know Jesus? The Muslims aren't affecting my city." Even though most of us do not have much contact with Muslims, they still have an impact on us. Many Muslims have a strategy to take over the world, and yet many times Christians are tactically considering only one battle (the battle for our particular city) out of a vast global war.

If Christians continue to think and operate merely on a local tactical level, we will constantly be on the defensive, reacting to the advances of the enemy instead of setting the pace in the war. We will lose the battle for this generation around the world. However, if we think and act strategically by the power of the Holy Spirit, we will continue to see mighty victories for the kingdom of God.

The most obvious strategy is to plant the gospel in every one of the 11,000 unreached people groups who have no access to the good news unless someone brings it to them. The focus of our world evangelization strategy must be to plant a strong church among each group that will grow to spiritual maturity and eventually evangelize the whole people group.

In his promise to Abraham God said, "I will bless you . . . and all peoples on earth will be blessed through you." God wants to bless you, but he also wants to bless 11,000 people groups through you. Whether you are a student, a nurse, or a construction worker, you can pray, you can give, and you can go.

The Importance of Prayer

Paul said, "The god of this age has blinded the minds of unbelievers, so that they cannot see the light of the gospel of the glory of Christ, who is the image of God" (2 Corinthians 4:4). Jesus said, "How can anyone enter a strong man's house and carry off his possessions unless he first ties up the strong man?" (Matthew 12:29).

The battle for souls will not be won merely by raising money and sending people. We can have the best strategies, equipment, and missionaries, but God is the only one who can take the blindness from people's eyes. That happens through unceasing prayer (1 Thessalonians 5:17). In other words, we must continue to pray for our particular assignment from the Lord until we see the victorious results.

In the early 1300s a Frenchman named Raymond Lull developed a burden for the Muslim world and went to live and preach among the Muslims in Bugia, Algeria. He was the first Christian missionary to the Muslims and after several years became the first Christian martyr in the region. Then, beginning in 1960, God led groups of Christians from around the world to go to Bugia for prayer and spiritual warfare. They felt God saying they were not to preach but to pray. Thirty years later every villager in Bugia became a Christian after Jesus appeared to each of them in dreams on the same night. The spiritual soil had been prepared through prayer, their blindness had been lifted, and the kingdom of God was able to advance and plunder the strong man's household.

Why are the nations of Senegal, Bhutan, Chad, and Azerbaijan so resistant to the gospel? One reason is that many of us don't know much about them, and we have not been praying for them. As a result, the people's eyes are still blinded by the god of this age. If we are going to be part of what God is doing in the world today, we need to pray specific prayers.

You can join in God's work by adopting one of these Gateway Cities for daily prayer, not stopping until the city is reached with the gospel. James 5:16 declares that "the prayer of a righteous man is powerful and effective." We may not be able to see all of the results of our prayers right away, but God has promised that they will be effective.

THE BATTLE
FOR THE GATEWAY CITIES

Viv Grigg

Director, Urban Leadership Foundation

In our world today there are nearly 500 cities of over one million people, and more than 220 of these could be classified as unevangelized. Billions of people have careened down rural roads into multiplying concrete highways to be emptied into the city and its slums. Almost all population increase now and in coming decades will be urban and urban migrant, as rural population growth remains static. The majority of these people will live in slums and squatter areas. The penetration of the cities and these urban poor communities define the target of missions for the twenty-first century. The future of missions is urban, especially among the poor.

Given the contexts of massive urbanization, globalization, and impoverishment of city populations, what is our goal in praying for cities? Let's look to the Master to find the answers. First, he came preaching the kingdom of God. Preaching, teaching, healing, and delivering were his primary activities. Jesus told his disciples in Matthew 9:37–38, "The harvest is plentiful but the workers are few. Ask the Lord of the harvest, therefore, to send out workers into his harvest field." We are to pray for laborers for the harvest who can do the same. Second, in Luke 4:18 Jesus declared that the focus of his mission and ours is to preach good news to the poor. We are to reach out to the poor and enter into their poverty, for that was the model of him who now intercedes for us.

The Cost of Penetrating Cities

Born into Hinduism, Ajay had been a language helper for a foreign Christian man. One day Ajay refused to give money for the *puja,* the celebration of worship of the goddess. Ajay had been reading the Bible, which said he was to worship only one God. He fled from the *bustee* (slum) and gave his life to Jesus.

During those days a train smashed into the bustee and two houses caught on fire. The people said these things happened because Ajay had turned against their goddess. The man to whom Ajay had taught language began praying for the city. One day in prayer, God spoke to him to take flowers and fruit to the families of those hurt by these events. When he did this, the people saw God come among them in a way they had never before experienced.

In another city, a slum was penetrated with the gospel at a great cost. One worker lost her hearing. Another became very sick. Fifteen other workers gave three to seven years of their lives, struggling with severe sicknesses and frequent demonic activities surrounding them. In support of these in-city workers, several hundred people were praying for them regularly. Today, as a result, ten slums in the city have emerging groups of worshiping Christians.

What will be the cost in the next city? It may be even greater. Every step must be bathed in prayer by hundreds of intercessors.

Cities and Spiritual Powers

Centers of tremendous power reside in the 10/40 Window. The city of Kolkata (Calcutta) is the servant of Kali (the Hindu goddess of death and destruction) and the center of Brahmanic Hinduism. Varanasi is one of India's holiest Hindu strongholds. Lhasa has mysterious Buddhist powers. Bangkok is the "city of the angels." In regular daily ceremonies, every portion of its land is dedicated to the spirits, for whom small houses are constructed. Toward Mecca, one-fifth of the world's population prays daily.

Penetrating these cities will be hard, persecution will be intense, and workers may face death. We must recognize the powers centered in the Gateway Cities, powers that control entire countries and regions, seeking to extend their influence over the whole earth. As more of the world's population moves into cities, we will face spiritual opposition at higher levels of intensity. In some cities, the depravity of man creates grotesque structures that enable the spiritual powers to wreak greater levels of destruction. Therefore, our task of reaching and transforming the cities will be increasingly difficult.

Strategic Points for Intercession

Through the proclamation of the gospel, the kingdom impacts the very structures of cities. Colossians 1:1–20 tells us that Christ is above all things and in control of the structures of the universe. He holds cities together. With that in mind, here are some strategic points for intercession.

1. *God has plans for the cities.* For each city God has a purpose and a battle plan. It is our task to discern this plan and then to walk with God in obedience. Listening to God and others, developing unity, and having the right timing are crucial factors. Every step in finding God's plan is the working of the Spirit as we walk with him. Every city is different. Every battle is different. We must seek God's guidance.

2. *Spiritual unity is key to spiritual warfare.* Linking believers around a common goal is a central element of reaching a city. This must be birthed by the Holy Spirit. The spiritual unity of believers is key to our spiritual power and effectiveness (see Acts 4:32–35). The Holy Spirit may not work significantly in a situation where he is grieved because of our disunity.

3. *Brokenness and reconciliation are essential.* If unity among believers in a city is not present, the first step is for them to come together in prayer and teaching until

there is mutual brokenness followed by reconciliation. By confessing their sins to one another, believers can begin to work together to transform their city.

4. ***Prayer movements promote unity.*** Prayer births visions of what God can do in the city and builds mutual trust and relationship. It is a common denominator around which many diverse Christian groups can work in unison. Citywide prayer, prayer walks, prayer marches, neighborhood prayer strategies, and concerts of prayer are some of the components of prayer movements.

5. ***Confession and humility free us from worldly powers.*** Many sins prevent effective intercession, and some, such as greed, stand out. Jesus taught that unless the grain of wheat dies, it does not bear fruit (John 12:24). By choosing to suffer with and befriend the poor, we are released from worldly powers of greed. This produces the character of the Spirit in us, enabling an outflow of his power and authority.

Finishing the Mission

The battle for the unreached peoples of the world will largely be fought in the cities. The resources to reach the cities with the message of the kingdom of God are available. The potential workers are available. Presence among the poor, proclamation of the good news, and continual prayer remain the keys to transform the lives of millions of people living in cities around the world, especially the Gateway Cities of the 10/40 Window.

KEY TO THE
PROFILES

The profiles of the 100 Gateway Cities are divided into four geographical sections: northern Africa, the Middle East, central Asia, and eastern Asia. At the beginning of each section the major unreached people groups are listed with their respective city. Each of the one hundred profiles follows a similar format to pack the maximum information into a limited space. The following explanation will enable you to use this information most effectively. When information for a category is unavailable, "unknown" is inserted.

Pronunciation Key: Under each city name is its English pronunciation. Emphasized syllables are highlighted in bold.

Meaning: The meaning of the city's name.

Country: City's country and, if applicable, province. An asterisk (*) identifies the city as a national or provincial capital.

Population: 2010 estimate for metropolitan area.

Living Standards: An indication of economic conditions in and around the city.

Religious Breakdown: Statistics are approximate. They illustrate the major religious groups active in the city as well as the relative strength of Christianity.

Status of the Church: Estimates of in-city churches and/or believers. Believers are classified as either indigenous (national) or expatriate (foreign).

Major Religious Sites: These are indicators of the city's spiritual and religious powers.

City Significance/History: A synopsis of the city's history and significance is provided. Further information can be found in travel guides, encyclopedias, and geographical dictionaries (gazetteers).

Prayer Points: These are specific areas for prayer, many of which come from in-city believers and workers. Each point is an excellent place to start in praying for the city. Additional information can be found in newspapers, magazines, missions periodicals, and prayer letters.

NORTHERN AFRICA

NORTHERN AFRICA
MAJOR UNREACHED PEOPLES

City	Peoples
Casablanca	Moroccan Arab, Shilha Berber, Riffian, Arabized Berber
Laayoune	Arab, Arabized Berber, Tahelhait Berber, Tamazight Berber
Nouakchott	Moor, Berber
Dakar	Wolof, Fulakunda, Tukulor, Serer
Banjul	Mandinso, Fula, Wolof, Jola
Bissau	Balanta, Manjako, Fulu, Mande
Conakry	Fula Jalon, Maninka, Susu, Yalunka
Bamako	Bambara, Fula Macina, Malinke, Tuareg, Bozo
Ouagadougou	Southern Senufo, Ivorian Malinke, Mossi, Tuareg
Algiers	Kabale Berber, Algerian Arab, Mozabite Berber, Hamayan Bedouin
Tunis	Tunisian Arab, Sahel Bedouin
Tripoli	Libyan Arab, Tripolitanian Arab, Cyrenaican Arab, Berber
Cotonou	Fon, Yoruba, Aja, Gun
Niamey	Zerma, Hausa, Sokoto Fulani
Kano	Hausa, Toroobe, Kanuri, Fulani
N'Djamena	Shuwa, Fula, Teda, Tubu
Khartoum	Beja, Guhayna, Gaaliin, Eastern Nuer
Djibouti	Issa Somali, Afar, Arab
Addis Ababa	Arusi Galla, Somali, Amhara, Tigrinya
Asmara	Tigrinya, Tigre & Mensa, Arab, Afar
Mogadishu	Somali, Sab, Digil, Rahanwiin

Meaning: "white house"
Country: Morocco*
Population: 3,267,000
Living Standards: Near 20% unemployment; thousands live in slums and shantytowns
Religious Breakdown:
98.1% Muslim
0.9% Christian
0.9% Nonreligious
0.1% Baha'i
Status of the Church: Mostly Roman Catholic, small Protestant communities; only 5% indigenous believers
Major Religious Sites: Hassan II Mosque (one of the world's largest mosques), Chleuh Mosque, Grand Mosque

Casablanca

(**kas**-uh-**blan**-kuh)

City Significance/History

The modern city of Casablanca originated from an ancient Berber hamlet called Anfa. Phoenician traders also used this site as a North African port.

At the beginning of the twentieth century, the French chose the small village of Casablanca for their economic center. The French protectorate lasted from 1912 to 1956. Today, with a population of over three million, Casablanca is by far Morocco's largest, most industrialized, and most modern city.

Islam is deeply rooted in the culture of Morocco. Most Moroccans firmly identify with Islam even if they do

Islam is deeply rooted in the culture of Morocco

not practice the religion. They proudly make their confession of faith, "There is no God but Allah, and Muhammad is his prophet." Devoted and nominal alike have an unquestioning faith in what they have been told, believing Islam is the only true faith.

Drawn by economic opportunities, both Arab and Berber migrants from around the country continue to pour into Casablanca. Most of these migrants, fresh from the countryside, are entering a completely different culture from the isolated rural villages.

PRAYER POINTS

1. Pray that people from all language groups would be able to hear the gospel.

2. Pray for unity and fellowship in the Holy Spirit. The few believers mistrust one another and fear that the other will turn them in to the government. This fear hinders believers from meeting together and growing.

3. Pray that increasing numbers will tune their radios to Christian broadcasts and that Casablancans receiving Bible correspondence materials will not be harassed.

4. Pray that the king and the government would recognize the indigenous church and that Moroccan church planters would be raised up.

5. Pray for missionary work to be permitted again and for tentmakers to be called.

Meaning: "water source"

Country: Western Sahara* (disputed territory)

Population: 195,000

Living Standards: Over 150,000 Sahrawis live in refugee camps in Algeria

Religious Breakdown:
99.4% Muslim
0.4% Nonreligious
0.2% Christian

Status of the Church: A small underground fellowship

Major Religious Sites: Central Mosque, Citadel and Mosque (at nearby Smara)

Laayoune

(lah-**yoon**)

City Significance/History

This oasis was little more than a small village until the Spanish developed an administrative, military, and provincial center in 1938. The Spanish were seeking to control their interest in the raw materials of Western Sahara, mainly ore.

Western Sahara, located just south of Morocco, is a disputed territory. Morocco claimed the land when Spain relinquished it in 1976, leading to a guerilla war and a longstanding dispute between Morocco and the Polisario Front, a Sahrawi-led independent movement. A cease-fire has been in place since 1991, but no resolution to the two groups' land claims has developed. Mauritania to the south also has interests in this land.

A cease-fire has been in place since 1991, but no resolution has developed

Although there is no official capital in this disputed territory, Laayoune (or El Aaiun) is the largest urban and political center of the territory. It is from here that the Moroccan government administers most of their Western Saharan affairs. The city also serves as an export center for phosphates from the Boukra mines.

PRAYER POINTS

1. The Sahrawi people are among the world's least reached. Pray that the gospel may be preached to them in their language and that they will come to know Jesus as the savior.

2. Pray that food and medical relief in the name of Jesus may be administered to the Sahrawis suffering in exile.

3. Pray for protection over the small group of Christians who must meet secretly.

4. Pray for the Moroccan Christian converts who have relocated to the city because of job opportunities.

5. Pray that the people may determine their own government and that the unstable political situation may be resolved.

Meaning: "place of the winds"

Country: Mauritania*

Population: 776,000

Living Standards: Tens of thousands of people live in slums

Religious Breakdown:
99.0% Muslim
0.5% Traditional Ethnic
0.4% Christian
0.1% Nonreligious

Status of the Church: A small persecuted church, mainly expatriate

Major Religious Sites: Ministry of Islamic Orientation, Boutilimit Home (nearby pilgrimage site)

Nouakchott
(nwahk-**shot**)

City Significance/History

Because of its coastal locale and mild climate, this small village of adobe huts was chosen to be the capital of the Islamic Republic of Mauritania in 1960. By 1964 the population (12,300) started to grow and has increased to almost one million.

In Mauritania a major ethnic line has been drawn. Arab-Berbers (Moors) make up the majority of the population to the north, and black Africans (Afro-Mauritanians) live in the south.

Northern and southern Africans are being forced from the sahel, the region on the edge of the Sahara Desert, because the ever-enlarging Sahara is depleting the sahel's water sources.

Storms blow sand, forming dunes that cover the fragile, drought-stricken land. As a result, cities like Nouakchott must support a fast-growing refugee population.

On the city limit, residents of cardboard shantytowns now make up two-thirds of the total metro population. Overpopulation is causing great deforestation, which in a short time will result in desertification. Goats, camels, and cows seek survival in piles of trash. Desert sandstorms rage two hundred days per year and now blow on the streets of Nouakchott, one of the newer capitals in the world.

PRAYER POINTS

1. Pray that Islamic law (*sharia*) would be overturned and that freedom of religion would be established.

2. Pray for believers to be strengthened in the face of persecution and the threat of death. Pray for steadfast, godly leaders to be raised up.

3. Pray for Muslims to realize the truth of Jesus and be given the grace and courage to follow Jesus as Lord.

4. Pray that Christian humanitarian relief to the drought-stricken would show God's love and that the physical needs of the poor would be met.

5. Pray that more radio broadcasts in Hassaniya Arabic will be produced. Pray for the translation of a Hassaniya Bible.

Meaning: "tamarind tree"
Country: Senegal*
Population: 2,856,000
Living Standards: Slums and many seasonal migrants
Religious Breakdown:
84.4% Muslim
9.0% Christian
6.0% Traditional Ethnic
0.4% Nonreligious
0.2% Other
Status of the Church: Mostly Roman Catholic; only a few of the ethnic groups have churches
Major Religious Sites: Grand Mosque

Dakar
(dah-**kahr**)

City Significance/History

Many of the capital cities in Africa were developed by European ruling powers in the nineteenth century or earlier. At this time African seaport cities became economic centers, trading everything from peanuts to slaves.

Dakar has the most strategic location of them all. It was from Goree Island that three million slaves were shipped. As the westernmost point in Africa, Dakar is the best departure port for South America, making it a strategic military location for the Atlantic south of the equator, and a trade hub for West Africa.

Founded by the French in 1857, Dakar was named the capital of French West Africa. This beautiful city is economically wealthy compared to the rest of the country. As the national railway terminal, it fosters significant trade and revenue.

Many poor villagers come to the city to sell vegetables and fruits, or move there in hopes of making money to send back to the village. A missions strategy has developed from this kind of migration. By reaching large, significant cities it might be possible to reach all the ethnic groups in the whole country. If one of these migrants hears the good news of Jesus, he or she might take Jesus back to the village.

PRAYER POINTS

1. Pray for workers to evangelize the many ethnic communities living in the city. Most of these communities need separate church-planting efforts because they speak different languages.

2. Pray for continued religious tolerance by the Muslim government. The freedom to witness without fear of persecution is rare in Muslim countries.

3. Pray that a spiritual breakthrough will occur among the powerful Sufi brotherhoods, who are some of the most devout Muslims in the country.

4. Pray that the lifestyle of nominal Christians would be transformed to better reflect a life in Christ.

5. Pray that young people who have moved to Dakar for education and employment would be reached with the gospel. Pray for students at Dakar University.

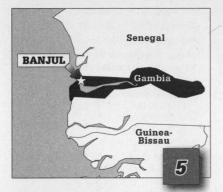

Meaning: "bamboo island"
Country: Gambia*
Population: 357,000
Living Standards: Subsistence living for many
Religious Breakdown:
85.3% Muslim
7.6% Traditional Ethnic
5.6% Christian
0.9% Baha'i
0.6% Nonreligious
Status of the Church: Mainly Roman Catholic; some Protestant, Anglican, and independent churches
Major Religious Sites: New Banjul Central Mosque

Banjul
(bahn-**juul**)

City Significance/History

Banjul was nothing more than a cluster of mud huts until African slave labor arose in more developed countries. The British changed this village into a large trading post.

Alex Haley's book *Roots* traced Kunta Kinte's homeland to Gambia. It was in the village of Juffure where he was captured and taken to the port of Banjul for transport to North America.

Banjul, located at the mouth of the Gambia River, became a destination where slaves were transported. The 700-mile-long river allowed slave traders to capture slaves far inland and

Banjul became a destination where slaves were transported

transport them easily for auction and deportation in Banjul. Once on the ships, they went to slave plantations throughout the world.

Today Banjul, technically an island, has been connected to the mainland by a bridge. Its location has caused it to be demographically stagnant for years, and this has hurt the economy. However, the mainland suburbs around Banjul have grown extensively.

PRAYER POINTS

1. Pray that the church will reach out to the Muslim majority, particularly the Mandingo people of *Roots* fame.

2. Pray that Anglican and Methodist churches in Banjul will experience revival.

3. Pray for the ministries working with young people who have moved to Banjul seeking work.

4. Pray for continued freedom to proclaim the gospel in this Muslim land.

5. Prison ministry has produced many converts. Pray for more conversions and the reintegration of released prisoners into churches and communities.

6. Pray that the three Sufi brotherhoods would come to base their fellowship in the Holy Spirit.

Meaning: "It's finished"
Country: Guinea-Bissau*
Population: 409,000
Living Standards: Widespread poverty; city damaged by 1998–99 Civil War
Religious Breakdown:
43.0% Traditional Ethnic
41.0% Muslim
15.0% Christian
1.0% Nonreligious
Status of the Church: Mainly Roman Catholic; a maturing national church
Major Religious Sites: Avenue de Cintura Mosque, Roman Catholic Cathedral, Curadores Healing Houses (Animist)

Bissau
(bi-**sou**)

City Significance/History

Years ago, Muslim semi-nomadic herdsmen moved east into the flat lands and settled in Bissau. It became the capital of Portuguese Guinea, an overseas colony of Portugal. The Portuguese set up a fortified post here in 1765 to administrate their interests in the area.

Today Bissau is the center for commerce and industry, with exports of rice and coconut products. It is the largest city and capital of Guinea-Bissau.

Before Islam or Christianity entered the area, many of the African people lived in fear of, yet worshiped, different

The ancient beliefs mixed with whatever religion was laid over the top of them

spirits and fetishes (a practice called animism, spiritism, or traditional religion). These ancient beliefs mixed with whatever religion was laid over the top of them.

Therefore, strange animistic practices can be seen in people who are Muslim or Christians. Spiritual bondage is common among those who practice spiritism. Many people wear amulets and put symbols on their homes to avoid getting the "evil eye," a much-feared curse that many believe can kill a child.

PRAYER POINTS

1. Pray that animistic practices will be renounced by the believers and replaced with deep trust and faith in the power of Jesus.

2. Pray for Christians to have confidence in witnessing to Muslims.

3. Pray for financial blessing on the believers, whose poverty makes it difficult to support their pastors, and for more workers and national pastors to be raised up. Pray for outreach to the large townships on the outskirts of the city.

4. Pray against the growth and influence of new religious groups such as the Jehovah's Witnesses, Baha'is, Moonies, and New Apostolics.

5. Many young people have migrated from the interior seeking education and employment. Pray that they will find the gospel instead of materialism, disillusionment, and, increasingly, atheism.

Meaning: unknown
Country: Guinea*
Population: 1,645,000
Living Standards: Much poverty because of government corruption
Religious Breakdown:
  68.2% Muslim
  27.5% Traditional Ethnic
  4.0% Christian
  0.2% Nonreligious
  0.1% Buddhist
Status of the Church: Even mix of denominations; a growing number of national pastors/priests
Major Religious Sites: Grand Mosque

Conakry
(**kon**-uh-kree)

City Significance/History

Conakry began as a small fishing village on Tomba Island and has since developed into the country's main port, educational center, and capital.

After independence from France in 1958, Guinea embraced Marxist ideology. Christians suffered greatly under the Marxist, pro-Islamic government. The city went into decline, with the infrastructure almost completely collapsing. The streets became extremely dirty, with garbage everywhere.

A military coup in 1984 overthrew the Marxist regime and restored

Governments have struggled to bring recovery and economic progress

basic freedoms. Another military coup occurred in 2008. The governments have struggled to bring recovery and economic progress. The city has been the location of several anti-government protests and strikes. Presently there is religious liberty for Christian witness and missionary activity.

During the rainy season, Conakry may receive as much as twelve feet of rain. Iron and bauxite mining and exporting have permitted the city to grow slowly.

PRAYER POINTS

1. Pray for the economic recovery of the city—that jobs would be created and that the current government would be wise in the implementation of reforms.

2. Pray that freedom for Christian witness and missionary activity would continue.

3. Pray for the Christians to have a vision for evangelizing the Muslim majority.

4. Pray for the gospel to become established among the three dominant Muslim peoples—the Maninka, the Fula, and the Susu.

5. Pray for unity and cooperation among missions agencies and with the national churches.

Meaning: "crocodile pool"
Country: Mali*
Population: 1,708,000
Living Standards: Much poverty; inadequate water supplies and electricity
Religious Breakdown:
85.5% Muslim
10.0% Traditional Ethnic
4.4% Christian
0.1% Nonreligious
Status of the Church: Even split between Catholic and Protestant; converts from Islam face discrimination or persecution
Major Religious Sites: Great Mosque, Hamdallaye Islamic Center, Sorcery and Fetish Bazaar

Bamako
(**bam**-uh-koh)

City Significance/History

Five hundred years ago Bamako, situated on the fertile Niger River, was a Muslim trading center in the ancient Mali empire. When the French arrived in 1880, this metropolis had dwindled to approximately one thousand people. Today Bamako is the largest city in Mali and is growing rapidly. Mali is among the poorest countries in the world.

Musa and his thirteen-year-old younger brother, Mamadou, live in a small farming village some 300 kilometers from Bamako. This year they will find a ride on a truck going to the big city. This will cost money, but the amount they will receive for their fruits and vegetables will be at least double in the city. Last year Musa had learned from a Brazilian Christian man about new seeds that produce a greater harvest. He bought only a few because they were expensive. This year he plans to buy more. The man's words about the seeds had been true; they were worth the extra money.

This annual migration of about 100,000 people takes place as many young farmers leave their villages with goods grown during the rainy season and seek to sell them during the dry season. Many would like to stay in the city but cannot because jobs are very hard to find.

PRAYER POINTS

1. Pray for more workers to evangelize the city and start outreaches in the suburbs.

2. Pray that Christian radio stations will expand their audiences, that Christian programming on national TV will bear fruit, and that the literature ministry will flourish.

3. Pray that the Bambara people around Bamako will be evangelized and discipled.

4. Pray that Muslims who have a negative view of Christianity will come to see Jesus for who he is. Pray that Malian Christians will model Christlike behavior.

5. Koulouba Hill overlooking the city is noted both as a hiding place for thieves and as the site of the presidential palace. Pray that corruption and thievery would cease and that all who are leading from atop this hill would be overcome by the gospel of Christ.

Meaning: "place of the Ouaga people"
Country: Burkina Faso*
Population: 1,324,000
Living Standards: Much malnutrition, especially among children
Religious Breakdown:
40.0% Muslim
39.0% Christian
20.0% Traditional Ethnic
1.0% Nonreligious
Status of the Church: Recent growth; some Muslim converts
Major Religious Sites: Grand Mosque

Ouagadougou

(wah-guh-**doo**-goo)

City Significance/History

Historically, the city was the capital of the Mossi Kingdom. Since the rule of Naba Dulugu in the late eighteenth century, it has been predominantly Muslim. At nearby Crocodile Lake, homage is paid to the crocodile.

Thomas carries his sick son as he walks to the market. Skillets and pots hang on the walls of the corner store. Turning left he sees the religious man selling portions of scripture from the Koran. The man offers him one in a gazelle-skin pouch. Reasoning to himself, "Allah is great, but I need medicine today," he moves on.

Laughter fills the market, but fear grips Thomas's heart. His son has been sick for two weeks, and no one knows what to do. Just past the religious man, Thomas looks at a sign with pictures of a drink mixture of water, salt, and sugar. Being illiterate he fails to understand that it is a rehydration mix and moves on.

Finally he reaches the "bush doctors," who squat behind a cloth covered with snakes' heads, dried owls, and lions' tails. A broken antelope's horn pierces a heap of flint off to the left side. With almost his last money, he buys a little square of elephant hide as the prescription given by the bush doctor. Three days later his son dies of dehydration caused by diarrhea.

PRAYER POINTS

1. Pray that the power of idolatry, fetishism, and secret societies will be broken in Jesus' name.

2. Pray for a greater ministry to students, particularly to those at Ouagadougou University.

3. Pray that the church can be a healing agent in the midst of social upheavals and family breakdowns caused by urban migration.

4. Because of the high illiteracy rate, the need for audio scripture is great. Pray for workers and resources to produce these. Pray also for successful literacy programs.

5. Pray for continued growth in the church and for leaders to train and disciple the new converts.

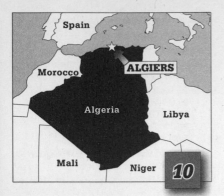

Meaning: "the islands"

Country: Algeria*

Population: 3,574,000

Living Standards: High cost of living, some very poor areas

Religious Breakdown:
97.5% Muslim
1.8% Nonreligious
0.7% Christian

Status of the Church: Small Protestant and Roman Catholic population; mostly private home fellowships

Major Religious Sites: Djemaa el Jedid (Fishermen or New) Mosque, Djemaa el Kebir (Great) Mosque, Sidi Abderrahman Mosque

Algiers
(al-**jeerz**)

City Significance/History

Algiers was an important commercial outpost first under Phoenicia and later under Carthage, Rome, and Byzantium. Pirates used this area as a protected location, and the Barbary Coast began to get a reputation in the sixteenth century.

The Ottoman Empire, based in Turkey, conquered much of North Africa. The Ottoman set up beys — provincial governors over its territories — and one was based in Algiers. The French controlled the area for the next 130 years, leading up to Algeria's independence in 1962.

Islamic fundamentalists have gained more political power

In the 1990s Islamic fundamentalists gained more political power, leading to a civil war between Islamist groups and the Algerian government from 1991 to 2002. The government defeated the groups, but Islamic terrorist groups are still active in Algeria.

The practice of religions other than Islam is officially prohibited, although some churches have been able to assemble without government interference. Other Christians assemble in private homes. Evangelism is prohibited.

PRAYER POINTS

1. Pray for peace in the city and safety for the innocent. Pray that terrorist groups will turn from their ways and come to know the Savior.

2. Pray for Muslim women as more Islamic laws are placed on them. These laws restrict their freedom and make them second-class citizens. Pray for Christian marriages and godly families to be raised up.

3. Pray for the foreign population. In past years Islamic fundamentalists have targeted foreigners with violent acts. Missionaries have been affected and forced to leave.

4. Pray for the security of Berber and Arab Christians and the underground churches. Some have received death threats, and murders occur regularly in the city.

Meaning: unknown

Country: Tunisia*

Population: 2,100,000

Living Standards: No major slums, much unemployment

Religious Breakdown:
98.9% Muslim
0.9% Christian
0.2% Nonreligious

Status of the Church: Mainly Roman Catholic; some Tunisian evangelicals

Major Religious Sites: Zitouna Mosque and Islamic University, Rue Jemaa es Zituna Mosque

Tunis

(**too**-nis)

City Significance/History

Tunis originally sprang up as a Phoenician trading post nearly three thousand years ago. The ancient Carthaginian Empire was centered in Carthage—now an archaeological site outside Tunis. Child sacrifice was practiced by the people to worship Baal. Among the ruins, a graveyard for children and an altar where children were sacrificed have been unearthed. On the Bougarneen mountain outside of Tunis it is reported that child sacrifice still takes place.

After Carthage was destroyed by the Romans in 146 BC, Tunis grew as a Roman, Byzantine, and finally an Arab city. In 1962 French rule ended.

The government of Tunisia has fought to keep the country out of the hands of Islamic fundamentalist groups. They declared the Islamist group Ennahdha illegal and charged some members with treason. Unemployment and a sluggish economy have not helped the government, but they are seeking to enhance trade with industrialized nations.

Islam is the state religion of Tunisia, but religious freedom is provided for by the constitution. Proselytizing, however, is prohibited, and Muslims who convert to another religion such as Christianity are discriminated against and are denied certain rights.

PRAYER POINTS

1. Pray against the spirit of materialism that strongly grips the people's hearts. Individually and nationally, the highest priority is peace and prosperity.

2. Lift before the Lord the lasting effects of Baal worship, asking him to remove whatever spiritual strongholds might still remain.

3. Pray that God would use economic hardships to draw Tunisians to himself.

4. Pray for unity as well as new vitality and growth in the small Christian community.

5. Pray that God would reveal his holiness to the Tunisians so that they will be convicted of sin and realize their need to have a relationship with God through his Son.

6. Pray that the government would ease its restrictions on evangelism, allowing individuals freedom to investigate the gospel.

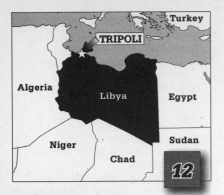

Meaning: a natural abrasive

Country: Libya*

Population: 2,322,000

Living Standards: A growing economy and increased standard of living

Religious Breakdown:
95.6% Muslim
3.8% Christian
0.3% Buddhist
0.2% Nonreligious
0.1% Other

Status of the Church: Mainly Orthodox; a handful of Libyan believers

Major Religious Sites: Gurgi Mosque, Karamanli Mosque

Tripoli
(**trip**-uh-lee)

City Significance/History

Also called Tarabulus, Tripoli is a seaport first settled by the Phoenicians. One of the first items exported was tripoli, a light-colored, very fine powder used as an abrasive or for polishing. Desert traders also brought gold, ivory, ebony, dates, and other goods by camel caravans to Tripoli.

History has proven to be very violent for the city and people of Tripoli, with one conqueror after another fighting for this city. The Phoenicians were replaced by the Romans, then the Vandals, Byzantines, Arabs (who brought Islam to the area), Spanish, Turks, Italians, and British. Libya became an independent kingdom in 1951.

In 1969 modern-day Libya was established through a coup that placed Muammar Qadhafi in power. He has traditionally balanced the government between Islamic fundamentalists who desire a stronger Islamic state and rivalries within the regime itself. Tripoli is the capital of Qadhafi's military regime.

Libya has been a strong force behind the spread of Islam in other nations and for international terrorist activities. It is also the headquarters for the World Islamic Call Society, a major Islamic mission organization. Due to government restrictions, church denominations in Libya are limited to one place of worship per city.

PRAYER POINTS

1. Pray that the terrorist activity emanating from Tripoli would stop and that the financial support of terrorism would end.

2. Pray that evangelism would again be allowed in Libya and that church denominations will be allowed to meet in multiple locations.

3. Pray that radio programming beamed into the city would find a responsive audience and that many would turn to the Lord.

4. Pray that foreign Christians working in Tripoli would have wisdom, boldness, and protection as they witness to Libyans. Many of these workers can share their faith only with people they trust, who will not turn them into the police.

5. Pray that God would redirect the evangelistic plans of the World Islamic Call Society and bring many to himself who would otherwise be missionaries for Islam.

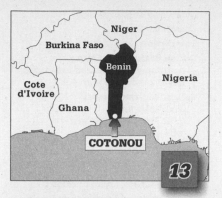

Meaning: unknown
Country: Benin*
Population: 841,000
Living Standards: Population growth has offset growing economic opportunities
Religious Breakdown:
38.0% Traditional Ethnic
37.0% Christian
24.7% Muslim
0.2% Nonreligious
0.1% Baha'i
Status of the Church: Large Roman Catholic, Protestant, and independent church populations; some mixing with traditional beliefs
Major Religious Sites: Cotonou Cathedral, Central Mosque

Cotonou
(**koh**-toh-**noo**)

City Significance/History

The countries just south of the Sahara Desert were the nearest place for developing nations to receive cheap slave labor. Thus port cities grew, slave ships came and went, and African families were torn to pieces. Cotonou was one of the centers for the deportation of slaves. The coast in this area became known as the "Slave Coast."

Today, although neighboring Porto Novo is the official capital of Benin, most government and diplomatic functions occur in Cotonou. In 1960 Benin received its independence from France.

The cult of voodoo continues to keep people in spiritual bondage

In 1991 democracy replaced the Marxist government that had ruled for over a decade, and free elections have taken place since.

The government supports religious freedom for all faiths, and the church has experienced considerable growth. The cult of voodoo was born in Benin, and it continues to keep people in spiritual bondage. Some professing Christians and Muslims also practice voodoo.

PRAYER POINTS

1. Pray for complete restoration and healing of a place that was devastated by the sinful actions of nations that enslaved its people.

2. Pray that Benin's government will continue to support religious freedom and that its future leaders will follow Christ.

3. God is more powerful than all traditional religions and voodoo practices. Pray that God would reveal his mighty power in Cotonou and break the hold of animism.

4. Pray for workers to reach the unevangelized Muslims who make up over 20% of the urban population.

5. Pray for continued growth in the church and for more leaders to be trained as pastors to shepherd the people.

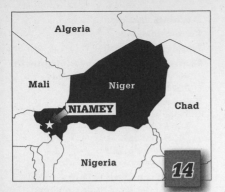

Meaning: unknown

Country: Niger*

Population: 1,027,000

Living Standards: Slum communities, strained resources because of rural migration

Religious Breakdown:
91.4% Muslim
6.5% Traditional Ethnic
2.0% Christian
0.1% Other

Status of the Church: Mix of Roman Catholic, Protestant, and independent denominations

Major Religious Sites: New Grand Mosque, Old Grand Mosque

Niamey

(nee-**ah**-may)

City Significance/History

Niamey began as an agricultural village where three different ethnic groups—the Maouri, Zerma, and Fulani—formed a village on the banks of the Niger River.

At the turn of the twentieth century, Niamey became a small French military outpost to help navigators on the river and to control the inland interests of France. Its river location allowed for travel into many of the surrounding countries. For many people in West Africa, the Niger River is a source of life and income.

In 1930 the city had about two thousand people. This little village on the river has grown to over four hundred thousand people today. It is the capital and largest city in Niger, which is one of the poorest countries in the world. The country's government provides few services to its people, who survive on a subsistence basis.

Drought has forced many people to move to Niamey from rural areas

Drought has forced many people to move to Niamey from rural areas and other neighboring countries. These people have brought an international flavor with them and turned Niamey into a trading center.

PRAYER POINTS

1. Pray for workers to evangelize this Muslim city that is open to the gospel.

2. Pray that God would supernaturally reveal himself to students at the Islamic University near Niamey.

3. Emigration and migration has forced rapid growth in the city. Pray that the needs of the poor would be met and that Jesus would be known.

4. Pray that young Christians would be able to find work and not be pressured to abandon their faith in exchange for job security.

5. Pray that God would raise up more Christian leaders from the local population.

6. Many are attracted to Christianity but fear possible persecution. Pray for a lessening of persecution, strength to believe, and boldness to live for Christ.

Meaning: unknown

Country: Nigeria, Kano State*

Population: 3,393,000

Living Standards: Many live in mud block homes with poor nutrition, sanitation, and health

Religious Breakdown:
78.0% Muslim
13.0% Christian
8.7% Traditional Ethnic
0.3% Other

Status of the Church: Many Christians left the city after the establishment of Islamic law in 2000

Major Religious Sites: Central Mosque, New Mosque

Kano
(**kahn**-oh)

City Significance/History

In the middle of Nigeria there is an imaginary line drawn. The forces behind it have spiritual roots. To the north of this line the knowledge of Christ is almost nil. From the line south, amazing church growth has occurred. The capital, the largest city, and most churches are in Nigeria's south.

Kano, Nigeria's second largest city, is the oldest city in West Africa. It has been a commercial center in the region for hundreds of years. Camel caravans have been replaced by trucks, but it is still a lively city.

Some miles away from Kano, the tall, white minarets and green tile dome of the mosque tower appear above the heat waves lifting off the desert sand. The interior part of the city is surrounded by a wall. Inside this wall on Friday, the holy day, fifty thousand Muslims will bathe, remove their shoes, and enter the mosque to pray.

As the mosque gets closer, this ancient Hausa city takes shape. A few shade trees cover one-story adobe homes. The walls are thick to give warmth in the winter, and bring needy relief from the sun during the summer. Streets run in all directions, twisting and turning as the city continues to grow, as homes are being built out of the earth around them.

PRAYER POINTS

1. Pray that Christian ministries may be established in Greater Kano, the Muslim city center that is separated by a wall. Pray that the spiritual wall that it symbolizes may be broken down in the hearts of the Kanawas.

2. Pray that the city's high divorce rate will be lowered. This is caused by forced marriages of girls ages ten to twelve, who become pregnant and damage their reproductive organs at delivery. Husbands then divorce their sterile wives.

3. Pray for an end to the burning of churches and the persecution of Christian leaders.

4. Pray that Christian professionals would develop effective cross-cultural evangelistic strategies such as medical service and well drilling.

5. In Kano and other northern cities in Nigeria, strict Islamic law is in place. Pray for missionaries to be raised up among the Issawa, Maguzawa, and Bade tribes.

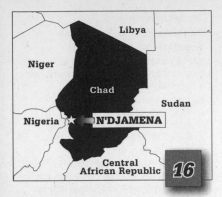

Meaning: "we rested"

Country: Chad*

Population: 1,127,000

Living Standards: Many live in severe poverty with lack of clean water and sanitation

Religious Breakdown:
53.0% Muslim
30.3% Christian
15.9% Traditional Ethnic
0.8% Baha'i

Status of the Church: About one hundred churches of various denominations

Major Religious Sites: Grand Mosque, King Faisal Mosque and School

N'Djamena

(en-jah-**may**-nuh)

City Significance/History

Lake Chad, once one of the largest lakes in the world, has been shrinking over the past one hundred years because of droughts, the growth of the Sahara, and irrigation projects. N'Djamena, the capital city of Chad, is located southeast of Lake Chad on the Chari River.

For people like the Muslim Tuaregs, growing vegetables on one small section of land does not satisfy their nomadic nature. The vast lands of northern Chad, not the city, are their dwelling. But famines have forced cultural changes, and in recent decades N'Djamena has experienced rapid growth because of famine and the hope of a better life in the big city. However, even the city has felt the effects of economic decline.

The city was the location of two recent battles

The government created feeding centers on the routes people were taking to the capital in order to control the growth of the city. These centers have become cities in themselves. Cotton is one of the main exports of the country. In 2004 the country began exporting oil.

In 2006 and 2008 the city was the location of two battles, in which rebel forces attempted to take over the city but were defeated by the Chadian military.

PRAYER POINTS

1. Pray for the training of pastors and evangelists at the Shalom Higher School of Theology—that the believers' fear of witnessing to Muslims would disappear.

2. Pray that the city will cease being a center for propagating Islam and instead be a center for propagating the gospel.

3. Pray for the poor living around N'Djamena. Many people do not have enough food.

4. Pray that those coming to N'Djamena for work would be receptive to the gospel and that Christians who must live with Muslim relatives would not convert to Islam.

5. Pray that the suspicion and animosity among the hundred-plus ethnic groups would find unity in the reconciling power of Jesus Christ.

6. Pray for the development of the New Testament and more Christian literature in the Chad Arabic dialect.

Meaning: "elephant's trunk"

Country: Sudan*

Population: 5,185,000

Living Standards: 2.8 million displaced people not officially counted in Sudan's population

Religious Breakdown:
66.0% Muslim
23.0% Christian
10.0% Traditional Ethnic
1.0% Nonreligious

Status of the Church: Growth among relocated southerners; a few Muslim converts

Major Religious Sites: Hamed al Niel Mosque, El Kabir Mosque, Mahadi's Tomb

Khartoum
(kahr-**toom**)

City Significance/History

The spread of Christianity in the early centuries followed trade routes. It remained north of the Sahara Desert and along the Mediterranean Sea, but was able to penetrate into Sudan because of the Nile River.

The White and Blue Nile rivers joined together to make a fertile agricultural zone where life was pleasant and crops grew well. Established nearby was Soba, the capital of the Christian kingdom of Nubia (c. 580), not far from present-day Khartoum. By the fourteenth century an active Christian kingdom was almost extinct as Islam grew. During the nineteenth century Khartoum became an export location for slaves and ivory.

The silver-domed mosque and minarets mark this Islamic capital. Islam has been growing in the north of Sudan as Muslim holy men lead the country into *sharia* (Islamic) law. This law is forced on the Muslims and non-Muslims alike.

Famine and war have caused much death and hardship for the Sudanese people. Many non-Muslims have sought help in Khartoum but have been banished to the harsh southern desert. Millions of internally displaced people have settled around Khartoum. Aid sent to Sudan rarely reaches the needy. The suffering has heightened as the government has stymied relief efforts.

PRAYER POINTS

1. Pray for peace and that relief shipments can get to the people. Pray that Christian relief agencies can get in and be protected from hostile political forces.

2. Pray that workers can train and teach local leaders. Pray that Sudanese Christians will then evangelize and disciple new believers to carry on the gospel, thus helping new churches to grow.

3. Pray for Bible translation work to continue and for more translators; pray also for workers in literacy training.

4. Pray that the government will treat non-Muslims fairly and will provide displaced people with the aid they need.

5. Pray for financial resources to rebuild the church and for strength to withstand suffering.

Meaning: "queen of the sands"

Country: Djibouti*

Population: 596,000

Living Standards: 60% unemployment

Religious Breakdown:
93.7% Muslim
5.0% Christian
1.2% Nonreligious
0.1% Other

Status of the Church: Majority of Christians are French; a few small indigenous fellowships

Major Religious Sites: Jamac Mosque, Altixad Islamic School

Djibouti
(jeh-**boo**-tee)

City Significance/History

Water has dictated the lives of traditionally nomadic shepherds. Two main peoples, the Somalis and Afars, have wandered the desert for centuries seeking water for their herds. At times wars have started over this valuable resource. Under the desert, water can be found, but digging for it is costly.

In a country where over one-third of the people are illiterate, Hassan, one of his father's fifteen children, was able to take a giant step forward. As a boy he wandered with his nomadic family; however, he had since learned to read, which set him apart. He managed to go to college and now teaches in Djibouti. People like Hassan are the future leaders of this small nation in eastern Africa.

Djibouti, the only major city in the country, rests on the west side of the strait of Bab el Mandeb, "Gate of Sorrow." This strait separates the Red Sea and the Indian Ocean.

Economically, Djibouti has been hard hit. Unemployment is approximately 60%. Many immigrants and refugees have come to the city, inhibiting economic growth in an area with few natural resources and little industry. Although the first multi-party presidential election was held successfully in 1999, the government struggles to improve conditions in the country.

PRAYER POINTS

1. With unemployment so high, many people are living in poverty. Pray that more jobs will become available.

2. Pray that peace and stability between the Somalis and Afars will continue (a civil war between the groups ended in 2001), and that there will be continued openness to a Christian presence.

3. Pray for the missionaries laboring in the extreme living conditions of this hot, harsh desert climate.

4. Pray for converts to result from ministries involved with education, public health, agriculture, literature, and youth work.

5. Pray for the effective use of literacy programs and the Scriptures in Somali and Afar.

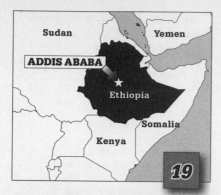

Meaning: "new flower"

Country: Ethiopia*

Population: 3,453,000

Living Standards: Shantytowns surround the city

Religious Breakdown:
70.0% Christian
24.0% Muslim
5.8% Traditional Ethnic
0.2% Other

Status of the Church: Ancient Orthodox church; growing Evangelical and Pentecostal churches

Major Religious Sites: Grand Mosque, Ethiopia Orthodox Church, Menelik Mausoleum

Addis Ababa

(**ah**-dis **ah**-bah-bah)

City Significance/History

The Amharic people of Ethiopia's highlands built their capitol at Addis Ababa, a natural 8,000-foot-high fortress. From there they could control most of the lowlands.

The "king of kings," Haile Selassie, had reigned almost fifty years as the 225th emperor, claiming descent from the union of the Queen of Sheba and King Solomon of Israel. Ethiopians believe that the ark of the covenant is in Ethiopia. The Christian church started when the Ethiopian eunuch encountered Philip in Acts 7.

The Ethiopian Marxist revolution of 1974 moved the whole country from the thirteenth century into the twentieth century through seventeen years of excessive violence. Drought and political extremism allowed one of the greatest famines in modern history to kill more than a million people. The Derg (communist) political party used extreme fear and coercion to keep people under control. Today this party has been outlawed. Developments have taken place with modern buildings now rising behind the mud-walled huts.

Thousands cannot find work

Addis Ababa is the headquarters for both the African Union and the UN Economic Commission on Africa.

PRAYER POINTS

1. Pray that students in the Bible schools and seminaries would be filled with the Holy Spirit and anointed to preach the gospel powerfully.

2. Pray that the government could lead the country into economic recovery and a higher quality of life for the people.

3. Pray that the poor street children, beggars, and handicapped war veterans would receive food and the gospel.

4. Pray for God to raise up strong family structures that will be a model for Christian homes and marriages.

5. Thousands of high school graduates and other youth cannot find work. Pray for the creation of jobs.

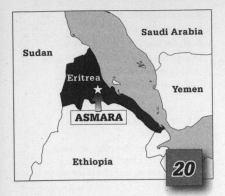

Meaning: union of four city names
Country: Eritrea*
Population: 1,147,000
Living Standards: Poverty high, but stabilizing
Religious Breakdown:
51.0% Muslim
45.4% Christian
2.9% Nonreligious
0.7% Other
Status of the Church: Mostly Orthodox; Protestants face government persecution
Major Religious Sites: Anwar Mosque

Asmara
(as-**mar**-uh)

City Significance/History

At the edge of a high plateau rests Asmara, a once beautiful Italian-built city, and now the capital of Eritrea. A large university was founded here in 1958.

Ethiopia claimed Eritrea as part of the Ethiopian Empire. For over thirty years Eritrea sought independence from Ethiopia through violence and political wars. Drought and war led to a famine that killed many.

In 1993 independence was granted and a new country was formed, but the beautiful Italian city had been marred by machine guns and mortars.

Drought and war led to a famine

Since then, reconstruction of the land has taken place. Roads destroyed in the war were patched, and crops have grown. In recent years the city has been able to double crop production, allowing for a reduction in foreign aid.

Having fought and died together has allowed Muslims and Christians to work together toward building a new country. Dropping ethnic differences has also permitted stability and a national identity. Although not affecting Asmara, land disputes between Eritrea and Ethiopia continue.

PRAYER POINTS

1. Pray for Protestants who are persecuted by the government. Pray for complete religious freedom in the country.

2. Coptic Orthodox and evangelical Christians have met and worshiped together. Pray for increased unity and for revival to enter these churches.

3. Pray for Muslim converts among the Tigre, Afar, Beja, and Saho peoples.

4. Pray for the protection and success of Christian missionaries and indeginous theology students and pastors.

5. Pray for finances to enable churches to rebuild and repair facilities damaged by fighting.

Meaning: unknown

Country: Somalia*

Population: 1,500,000

Living Standards: Violence and drought have caused great poverty

Religious Breakdown:
97.3% Muslim
2.5% Christian
0.1% Traditional Ethnic
0.1% Other

Status of the Church: Little growth in the past one hundred years; a few Somali believers

Major Religious Sites: Fakhr al-Din Mosque, Great Mosque

Mogadishu
(moh-guh-**di**-shoo)

City Significance/History

War, drought, devastation—a cycle of life for Saphia. She ran out of food, and her two camels and goats died as the ground turned to dust. Eight months pregnant, she decided not to flee with her family to Ethiopia. Instead, Saphia moved to a refugee camp outside Mogadishu, where the streets became battle zones. Daily her husband sought food and work in the city.

One day Saphia's husband was standing in a food line when a machine gun mounted on the back of a truck turned the corner and fired on the crowd. He died

> *One of the most dangerous and lawless cities on the globe*

on the street. Saphia and her baby survive only on what Saphia receives from the food handouts from the refugee workers.

Considered one of the most dangerous and lawless cities on the globe, Mogadishu has been a zone of intense fighting since 1990, when rebel groups first took over the city. In 2006 an Islamic militia defeated the rebel warlords but were in turn defeated by Ethiopian troops in 2008. Over half the population fled the city, whose future remains uncertain.

PRAYER POINTS

1. Pray that the Somali government would be stabilized and would bring order and justice to the city and nation.

2. Pray that the poor would receive the food and care they need.

3. Pray that the streets would be peaceful and safe, not battle zones.

4. Pray that Christian relief workers can effectively communicate the love of Christ as they distribute food and medicine.

5. Pray for protection and growth of the underground Somali church. Pray also for new opportunities for missionaries in the country.

MIDDLE EAST

MIDDLE EAST
MAJOR UNREACHED PEOPLES

City	Peoples
Mecca	Saudi Arab, Yemeni Arab, Filipino
Riyadh	Saudi Arab, Yemeni Arab, Pakistani
Sanaa	North Yemeni Arab, South Yemeni Arab, Somali
Muscat	Omani Arab, Balochi, Mahra
Abu Dhabi	Arab, Bedouin Arab, Irani Arab
Doha	Qatari Arab, Urdu, Baloch, Lebanese
Manama	Bahraini Arab, Palestinian Arab, Kurd, Malayali
Kuwait City	Arab, Kurd, Numerous Expatriates
Beirut	Lebanese, Palestinian Arab, Druze, Kurd
Tirana	Tosk, Gypsy, Vlash
Cairo	Bedouin, Arabized Berber, Egyptian Arab, Halebi Gypsy
Amman	Palestinian Arab, Jordanian Arab, Bedouin, Adygcy
Damascus	Bedouin Arab, Western Kurd, Turkmen, Palestinian Arab
Gaza	Palestinian Arab, Jew
Jerusalem	Arab, Jew, Bedouin
Tel Aviv	Jew, Palestinian Arab, Bedouin, Farsi
Istanbul	Turk, Persian, Levantine Arab, Turkish Kurd
Ankara	Turk, Persian, Turkish Kurd, Crimean Tatar
Izmir	Turk, Turkish Kurd, Persian
Baghdad	Iraqi Arab, Iraqi Kurd, Turkmen
Tehran	Luri, Mazanderani, Persian, Qashqai
Mashhad	Hazaras, Luri, Persian, Turkmen

Meaning: "the revered"
Country: Saudi Arabia
Population: 1,486,000
Living Standards: Poverty is rare among Saudis but prevalent among expatriates
Religious Breakdown:
99.99% Muslim
0.01% Christian
(The public or private practice of any religion other than Islam is prohibited.)
Status of the Church: An underground church of less than one hundred believers
Major Religious Sites: Grand Mosque, Ka'aba Shrine, Well of Zam Zam (said to be the well provided by God for Hagar and Ishmael)

Mecca
(**meh**-kuh)

City Significance/History

Mecca is the focal point of Islam. One-fifth of the world's population looks to this city as their most holy site. Devout Muslims pray facing Mecca five times a day; mosques all over the world are constructed with their front wall facing Mecca.

In 570 Muhammad was born in the city. Disillusioned with the pagan worship of many gods, Muhammad started to preach that there is only one god — Allah. After traveling around most of Arabia, he returned to Mecca shortly before he died.

At the center of the Grand Mosque's courtyard rests the Kaaba, a cubical structure made of granite. Islamic tradition says the Kaaba, a replica of God's heavenly home, was built by Abraham and Ishmael. (Muslims trace their lineage back to Abraham through Ishmael.) One corner of the Kaaba contains the Black Stone, which Muslims believe fell from heaven during the time of Adam and Eve.

The Koran states that every Muslim must make a pilgrimage (*Hajj*) to Mecca at least once in his life. On the ninth day of the month of Zhul Hijjah, according to the Muslim lunar calendar, millions of pilgrims pray on top of Mount Arafat just outside Mecca. This is the one of the world's largest religious gatherings. It is unlawful for any Christian to enter this holy Muslim city.

PRAYER POINTS

1. Pray that the Black Stone and the mystical powers behind it would be bound from captivating millions of Muslims.

2. Pray that the Muslims performing the annual *Hajj* would be disappointed with the commercialism of the city and that those seeking God would find Jesus.

3. Pray that the Islamic religious leaders and religious police would have miraculous encounters like Paul did on the road to Damascus. Without God working supernaturally, the city will not directly hear the gospel, except through radio.

4. Pray that the king and government of Saudi Arabia would allow Christians to work, reside, and worship openly in Mecca. Pray for strength for existing believers.

5. Pray for the neighboring city of Medina, Islam's second holiest city.

Meaning: "orchard" or "garden"

Country: Saudi Arabia*

Population: 4,856,000

Living Standards: Poverty is rare among Saudis but prevalent among expatriates

Religious Breakdown:
87.5% Muslim
10.5% Christian
1.0% Hindu
1.0% Other

Status of the Church: Significant number of expatriate Christians

Major Religious Sites: Imam University, King Faisal Islamic Center, over 2,000 mosques of different sizes

Riyadh
(ree-**yahd**)

City Significance/History

Tradition tells of the apostle Bartholomew wandering around Arabia with the message of the Savior. By the sixth century Christianity was firmly established; however, one hundred years later it was completely replaced by Islam, now the official Saudi religion.

A few oases marked the location of a small settlement at the heart of the dry rocky plateau. The coastal areas allowed for travel and trade, but few people ventured through Riyadh.

In 1902 Abdul Aziz recaptured the city from the Ottomans and forever changed its destiny. He designed it to be the national capital, but it still remained an isolated, mud-walled city of a few clay palaces. Jiddah on the Red Sea grew, but Riyadh saw little change.

Riyadh started toward modernization in the 1950s. Sand and mud walls gave way to marble palaces, mosques, and schools, such as Imam University, a world center of Islamic theology and outreach. Today Riyadh is one of the largest and most modernized cities in the Middle East.

The revenue from oil allowed for this explosion of growth. Even poor Saudis have benefited from oil, having moved out of the slum communities into housing provided by the government.

PRAYER POINTS

1. Pray that the king and the royal family would be moved by God to allow Christian worship. This is an important step toward more people hearing of Jesus.

2. Pray that tentmakers will be called to Riyadh and will spread the gospel through business in this modern metropolis.

3. Pray that the Wahhabi religious leader and the Mutawwa'in religious police, who are persecuting the church, would encounter the Lord Jesus.

4. Pray that God could break the stranglehold of Islam in educational institutions, which requires that 70 percent of all education be devoted to the study of Islam.

5. Pray for the underground church to grow strong and remain vibrant in the midst of persecution. Pray that they will endure with great joy.

Meaning: "fortified place"
Country: Yemen*
Population: 2,345,000
Living Standards: About one-third live in poverty
Religious Breakdown:
98.8% Muslim
0.6% Hindu
0.5% Christian
0.1% Other
Status of the Church: A few secret Yemeni believers
Major Religious Sites: Great Mosque, Al-Jami Al-Kabir Mosque, Salah ad-Din Mosque, al-Mutwakil Mosque, Muslim Brotherhood Headquarters

Sanaa
(sa-**nah**)

City Significance/History

The original name of the capital city of Yemen was Medinat Som, "City of Shem." Tradition holds that after the Flood, Shem, the son of Noah, built this city on the volcanic plain 2,225 meters above sea level.

By the turn of the first century, it had become a fortified city (it is still one of the largest and best preserved cities in the Arab world) along the great Incense Road leading to the Mediterranean. Myrrh and frankincense grew naturally and were valuable trade items.

South Yemen was formed in 1967 and became the world's only Arab Marxist

Tradition holds that Shem, the son of Noah, built the city

state. It signed a twenty-year friendship treaty with the USSR, which allowed Soviet troops in Yemen. North Yemen looked to the West politically.

The fall of communism in the world enabled Yemen to unite, and the Republic of Yemen was established in 1990 with Sanaa as the capital. The government has struggled to bring economic growth to the country—the poorest of the Arabian Peninsula. Riots have broken out in Sanaa because of the drop of oil prices and Islamic religious differences from north (Shiite) to south (Sunni).

PRAYER POINTS

1. The Muslim Brotherhood is very anti-Christian and is trying to stop all Christian activity. Pray that their efforts are unsuccessful.

2. Most residents have never heard the gospel because the city was sealed for over 1,300 years. Pray for fruit from Christian radio programs and boldness for the relief workers involved in health and educational projects.

3. Pray for strength for the believers who are under intense pressure from relatives and civil authorities to renounce their faith.

4. Pray that peace and reconciliation may prevail between the northern and southern factions in the past civil war. Pray that reforms will bring economic relief.

5. Pray against the spirit of fear that is especially intense because of the way the imam has exercised his authority.

Meaning: "place of falling" or "anchorage"

Country: Oman*

Population: 1,091,000

Living Standards: Generally good living standards because of oil

Religious Breakdown:
87.0% Muslim
5.5% Hindu
5.5% Christian
2.0% Other

Status of the Church: More than fifty fellowships of various denominations; mostly expatriate

Major Religious Sites: Khor Mosque, Ali Musa Mosque

Muscat
(**mus**-kat)

City Significance/History

Muscat has been a strategic seaport city for the last one thousand years. A mud fort, dwarfed by the volcanic mountains overhead, once provided protection for the capital city. The local people would fish, mine lime, or grow dates as their main income, but the sea was their connection to the outside world.

Sinbad, the famous sailor, sailed from Muscat to exotic places like India and China, trading lime, dates, and other goods from the Middle East for rice, coffee, and tea. Other ships stopped here before heading into the Persian Gulf or down the east side of Africa. Because of its location, the Portuguese captured Muscat and set up a regional stronghold in the 1580s. They were later replaced by the Al-Busaid Dynasty, who ruled as far as East Africa. By the mid-seventeenth century, Muscat was back in the hands of the Omani. In 1890 Samuel Zwemer established a medical mission work, which still continues.

Oil found in the desert enabled development in Muscat and surrounding towns during the twentieth century. The city has grown to include two adjacent cities—Muttrah and Ruwi. With diminishing oil resources, the economic future of Muscat is uncertain.

PRAYER POINTS

1. Pray for strength and boldness for the few indigenous believers and for new indigenous churches to be planted.

2. Pray that the sultan would allow Omani citizens freedom of religion.

3. Pray that radio broadcasts and literature distribution would reach the Muslim majority.

4. Pray that expatriate believers working in the city would show a Christian witness through their lifestyle and that their churches would have a positive impact on the surrounding communities.

5. Pray that ongoing medical missions work would show Christ's love to the people.

Qatar

ABU DHABI

U.A.E.

Oman

Saudi Arabia

26

Meaning: unknown
Country: United Arab Emirates*
Population: 897,000
Living Standards: Oil has turned poverty to fabulous wealth
Religious Breakdown:
75.0% Muslim
14.3% Christian
6.0% Hindu
2.0% Buddhist
2.7% Other
Status of the Church: Expatriates have churches; only a few Arab believers
Major Religious Sites: New Bazaar Mosque

Abu Dhabi

(**ah**-boo **dah**-bee)

City Significance/History

Originating from a sandy swamp, the whitewashed Al-Husn Palace in Abu Dhabi comes into view. A little over two hundred years ago, an ancestor of the present sheikh's family moved from the desert to the island and built a fort (which became the palace) around the sweet-water spring. Date farming and fishing provided the fort with food. Pearls opened the door for trade and export with India and Europe.

Up until the 1970s the city looked little different than in ancient days. It was the capital of the seven United Arab Emirates. (Abu Dhabi is also the name of the largest and richest of these emirates, and makes up over 90 percent of the emirates' total area.) But the growth and riches of oil were just starting to be felt. Today, caught between the sand dunes of Arabia and the waves of the Persian Gulf, the modern city has grown tremendously. It now appears as a cosmopolitan city of glass and concrete rising above the sand.

Eighty percent of the people living in Abu Dhabi are expatriates, coming from poorer Gulf states and places like India or Pakistan. Many of these expatriates work in servant roles that the native Arabs do not desire to do.

80% of the people are expatriates

PRAYER POINTS

1. Pray that the Supreme Council would allow freedom of religion for the citizens.

2. Pray that expatriate believers would have the opportunity to share the gospel with their Arab coworkers.

3. Pray for the establishment of an indigenous Arab church and for strong leaders to be raised up.

4. Pray that the people would see Christ's love demonstrated by the Christian medical agencies serving here.

5. Pray that videos, radio broadcasts, and literature would bear fruit in evangelizing all people groups.

Meaning: "half-circle"
Country: Qatar*
Population: 398,000
Living Standards: Great wealth; Asian workers live in poverty
Religious Breakdown:
83.0% Muslim
10.5% Christian
2.5% Hindu
4.0% Other
Status of the Church: Mostly expatriate
Major Religious Sites: Grand Mosque

Doha
(**doh**-hah)

City Significance/History

The expanding desert proved a hard place to live. Bedouins would move from one oasis to another, trying to make a living by trading dates and other goods. The coastal areas of the Persian Gulf allowed for a little more stability, providing food through fishing and a little income by diving for pearls. Doha was settled as these nomadic Bedouins chose to fish instead of wander the desert.

This small city remained poor and of little interest to the outside world for most of its history. Bahrain and Qatar have fought for the rights to the rich pearl beds, but otherwise little importance was given to Doha, Qatar's capital.

The British, a protector of Qatar until its independence in 1971, did not even have a representative in the country until after oil was found.

Just before World War II, Qatar was found to be oil rich. Ten years passed until oil production began. The whole country started to prosper because of the wealth of the black gold. The country also has some of the world's largest gas reserves. The pearl beds have dried up, but now oil rights have been the center of political squabbles between Bahrain and Qatar. Because of oil and natural gas, Qatar has the second-highest per capita income in the world.

PRAYER POINTS

1. Pray that some Qatari believers living abroad will return home and become the core of an indigenous church.
2. Pray that the emir would lift legal prohibitions against Christian evangelism.
3. Pray that the expatriate Christians working in Doha will be fruitful in their friendship evangelism.
4. Pray that evangelism utilizing radio and video might touch many lives.
5. Pray that the materialistic lifestyle produced by the great oil wealth would bring disillusionment and a renewed search for spiritual truth in Jesus.
6. Pray that students at Qatar University might be reached with the gospel.

Meaning: "place of rest"
Country: Bahrain*
Population: 166,000
Living Standards: Great wealth
Religious Breakdown:
  82.2% Muslim
  10.8% Christian
  6.0% Hindu
  1.0% Other
Status of the Church: Expatriates can worship freely; a few national believers
Major Religious Sites: Juma (Friday) Mosque, Beit al-Quran Islamic Center, Al Fateh Islamic Center

Manama
(muh-**na**-muh)

City Significance/History

Manama the money center, Manama where riches lay hidden. In the land of saltwater and desert sand, fresh water brings life. The city's wealth once richly flowed because of ample fresh water that helped date groves flourish, and also because of pearls that could be lifted out of knee-deep waters.

Now pearl divers have been replaced by urban oil workers. Wooden sailing ships stopping to fill their water tanks have become supertankers moving millions of barrels of oil.

It is expected that Bahrain will be the first Gulf state to run out of oil, but they are already planning ahead. The country is an international business center as well as a major exporter of aluminum.

In Manama, commercial banks were started when the oil revenues flowed. Because of this financial system, the city leads the way in banking in the Gulf and is the major banking center between London and Singapore. The economy is strong, and with investments under way, Manama will continue to be a leader in the Gulf.

Pearl divers have been replaced by oil workers

PRAYER POINTS

1. Pray that more people will listen to the Christian radio programs beamed into the city and that more Bibles will become available for distribution.

2. Pray that more Christian expatriates will come from Asia to be involved in evangelism and discipleship.

3. Pray that the emir and his advisers will allow evangelism among the Bahrainis.

4. Prayer for the growth and witness of Arabic-speaking evangelical congregations.

5. Pray for a spiritual harvest through the distribution of Christian literature and videos. Pray that Barhainis would recognize their need for a Savior.

Meaning: "small fort"
Country: Kuwait*
Population: 2,305,000
Living Standards: Significant wealth
Religious Breakdown:
  82.0% Muslim
  14.0% Christian
  3.0% Hindu
  1.0% Other
Status of the Church: Roman
  Catholic, Orthodox, and Protestant;
  mostly expatriates
Major Religious Sites: Grand
  Mosque, Shabaan Mosque

Kuwait City
(koo-**wayt**)

City Significance/History

From a small desert oasis making money from pearls and other traded goods, Kuwait City exploded as an oil producer. Five gates made entrance into the walled city possible. These walls, once protecting it from invasion, have crumbled. The city has expanded far past the old walls.

Oil wealth has turned Kuwait into one of the world's richest countries. Schooling, electricity, and water are all free to the Kuwaitis. Iraq's desire for more oil, supposedly to share with poorer countries, was their justification for military invasion in 1990–1991. When the Iraqis were driven out,

> *The oil fields were ablaze with five hundred wells burning out of control*

Kuwait City was free once again. The oil fields were ablaze with five hundred wells burning out of control. Black haze blocked the noonday sun. The Persian Gulf was full of oil. Damage to government and historical buildings was extremely high.

After the war, the government was quick to rebuild the city and normalize life. New hotels, malls, and office buildings sprang up quickly, and more are being built. Over $5 billion was spent to repair the oil infrastructure. The nation made another advance in 2009 with the first-ever election of four women to the National Assembly.

PRAYER POINTS

1. There is substantial freedom of worship in Kuwait, especially for foreigners. Pray that expatriate Christians will spread the gospel to the Muslims around them.

2. Pray that government officials will come to know Christ and will give support to churches and Christian mission organizations.

3. Pray for strength and boldness for Kuwaiti believers and for the establishment of an indigenous church.

4. Pray that the emir will grant full freedom of worship and witness to Kuwaiti and indigenous believers.

5. Pray that God will strengthen those Muslims who might consider converting to Christianity but are afraid of the repercussions.

Meaning: possibly "the wells"
Country: Lebanon*
Population: 1,941,000
Living Standards: Growing economy but areas of poverty especially in the south
Religious Breakdown:
53.7% Christian
40.3% Muslim
4.0% Nonreligious
2.0% Other
Status of the Church: Ancient Orthodox and Catholic churches; a few evangelical churches
Major Religious Sites: Harissa and Mt. Sherbal Maronite Monasteries

Beirut

(bay-**root**)

City Significance/History

A succession of different foreign powers have overrun and controlled Beirut throughout the past four millennia. The Assyrians, Greeks, Romans, Ottoman Turks, and French all used this city as a regional base. Most of these powers brought their gods with them.

For most of the twentieth century Beirut was a beautiful Mediterranean city and recognized as a principle banking and commercial center for the Arab world. Since the 1970s, however, Beirut has turned into a battle zone. Civil war broke out between Christians and Muslims in 1975, lasting until 1990. Also during this period, in 1982, Israeli forces fought against the Palestine Liberation Organization. A period of peace after the civil war was disrupted in 2006 when Israeli forces once again laid siege to the city, this time in response to Hezbollah attacks on Israel.

A margin of peace has returned to Beirut after decades of war in which Muslims and Christians brutally killed each other and international conflicts flared up. With the help of many international donors, the government has worked to rebuild the infrastructure of the city and country and bolster the economy. Tourism has increased in this city that was deemed the Paris of the Middle East after World War II and has since reestablished itself as a flourishing city.

PRAYER POINTS

1. Pray for reconcilation between Christians and Muslims who may still feel animosity because of the long civil war between them.

2. Pray that Christians would take advantage of a great openness among non-Christians to hear the gospel.

3. Pray that the youth would not be drawn into immorality and drugs, and that God would open doors for ministries to reach the youth.

4. Many families have suffered tremendously, losing members through violence and bloodshed. Ask God for comfort and consolation in the healing process.

5. Pray for the gospel to be preached on radio, on TV, and through videos and literature. Pray that the church would have a greater vision for media ministry.

Meaning: ancient name of Tuscany

Country: Albania*

Population: 538,000

Living Standards: Among the highest poverty rates in Europe

Religious Breakdown:
55.3% Muslim
39.5% Christian
5.0% Nonreligious
0.2% Other

Status of the Church: 57% Albanian Orthodox, 39% Roman Catholic, a few evangelical fellowships

Major Religious Sites: Ethem Bey Mosque, Enver Hoxha Memorial

Tirana
(ti-**rah**-nuh)

City Significance/History:

Paul, in Romans 15:19, reported that he had "proclaimed the gospel of Christ" in the region of Illyricum, which lay on the Adriatic Sea. Romans marched through this area on their way to Thessalonica and Constantinople. Other invaders in turn conquered, but were replaced by the Muslim Ottoman Turks. Albania became the only European country to be predominantly Muslim.

Sulejman Pasha Bargjini, an Ottoman Turk, founded Tirana in the seventeenth century, and it became Albania's capital in 1920. At this time there were about twelve thousand residents living in the city.

In 1944 communism gripped the country and radically changed it. For almost fifty years the strictest communism in the world closed churches and mosques, outlawed all religions, and sealed off the country from the outside world. Party propaganda shaped the lives of the people. The citizens were told that they were the richest people in the world. In reality, Albania was the poorest nation in Europe, with 60% unemployment and rapid inflation. Communism was overturned in the early 1990s.

Tirana is Albania's industrial and cultural center. Much of the city's buildings and roads are in disrepair, although restorative work is under way.

PRAYER POINTS

1. Pray for the poor as they struggle to live in a post-communist country, that God would use the economic struggles to bring many to Christ.

2. Pray that the influence and plans of Islamic nations to evangelize Albania would be thwarted.

3. Pray for the improvement of roads so that the gospel can be better transported to villages in the mountain regions.

4. Pray that the short-term evangelistic work will be successfully followed up with long-term work and discipleship, especially among young believers.

5. Pray for unity among the churches. Also pray that the church would find favor with the government.

Meaning: "the victorious"
Country: Egypt*
Population: 12,503,000
Living Standards: Many slums
Religious Breakdown:
  81.2% Muslim
  18.3% Christian
  0.5% Other
Status of the Church: Ancient Coptic Church; charismatic renewal taking place
Major Religious Sites: Ibn Tulun Mosque, El Ibn el Asn Mosque, Sultan Hassan Mosque, Al Azhar Mosque and University, El Hussein and Sayida Zeynab Tombs

Cairo
(**kai**-roh)

City Significance/History

The Bible tells of Jesus being taken to Egypt by his family because Herod was seeking to kill him. Tradition says he went to Cairo. After Jesus' resurrection, the old Roman fortress in Cairo became a Christian colony, a church, and eventually a convent. The ancient Coptic church also became centered in Cairo.

In the shadows of the ancient pyramids, Cairo rises from the desert floor as the largest city in Africa, having spread out along the Nile River over the centuries. The river provides life to a desert land. In the spring the desert heat increases. Sand blows and covers the streets of Cairo.

Islam entered the area early after Muhammad's death and has been a strong force ever since. Al-Azhar founded the oldest university in the world; it developed into the foremost Islamic theological center in 970. The crusaders tried to take Cairo by force, returning Christianity to the area, but were turned away by the Muslim defenders.

Life is hard for the poor. Living in overcrowded, run-down slums, millions are in the same situation, with no hope and seemingly no way out. They feel stuck and humiliated, yet their religious pride is still not broken.

PRAYER POINTS

1. Pray for the gospel to be presented to Muslims (most of whom are poor) in an understandable way and for culturally sensitive churches to be planted.

2. Pray that false worship involving homage to dead Muslim saints would be broken and that people would worship the risen Jesus.

3. Al-Azhar is the largest Islamic university in the world and sends out hundreds of Islamic missionaries annually. Pray that the students would be disillusioned with Islam and turn to Christ.

4. Pray for strong biblical faith in the Coptic and evangelical churches.

5. Pray for zealous Christian young people to be raised up to evangelize Cairo and Egypt. Pray for the few missionaries already being sent out from Egypt.

Meaning: "protected by Ammon"

Country: Jordan*

Population: 1,106,000

Living Standards: Growing economy but poorer eastern neighborhoods; many refugees

Religious Breakdown:
91.7% Muslim
5.0% Christian
3.0% Nonreligious
0.3% Other

Status of the Church: Mainly Eastern Orthodox and Roman Catholic; some Protestants

Major Religious Sites: King Hussein Mosque, Abu Darwish Mosque, King Abdullah Mosque

Amman

(ah-**mahn**)

City Significance/History

This ancient city dates back to the fourth millennium BC. In the Old Testament it is known as the Ammonite city of Rabbah. King David sent Uriah to this city to die in battle to cover David's sin with Bathsheba. At the city's capture, David completely destroyed the inhabitants by having them walk through an extremely hot furnace. David was, in some way, following a local custom. Molech, a deity to whom parents sacrificed their children by having them walk into or pass through a fiery kiln, was the god of the Ammonites.

As a fortified city in almost desert conditions, water is extremely important to life. Caravans of traders would pass through the city, exchanging goods and replenishing water. The city grew slowly over the seven hills of the area. The population exploded when it became the capital of Jordan (then called Transjordan) in 1921. Once a major hub of ancient travelers, it continues to be a crossroad in Jordan.

Jordan maintains the sacred Muslim shrines in Jerusalem and paid millions to regild the Dome of the Rock in 1994. West Amman has become an increasingly modern and liberal area with hotels, nightclubs, and bars. Prostitution is a problem.

PRAYER POINTS

1. Pray for the important work of Bible and literature distribution. Christian literature is sent from here throughout the Middle East.

2. Pray that the youth of the city will have the chance to hear and respond to the gospel. Pray that they will reject materialistic and carnal lifestyles.

3. Pray that godly and willing leaders will be raised up to serve growing churches and that finances to support them will be released.

4. Pray for churches and ministries to work together to spread the gospel of Jesus Christ in this predominantly Muslim city.

5. Amman is home to refugees from many countries. Pray for ministry to these groups, which face poverty and unemployment.

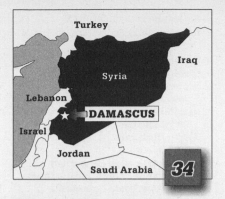

Meaning: named after Damshak, the city's founder

Country: Syria*

Population: 2,675,000

Living Standards: Economic boom since 2003; slums just outside city

Religious Breakdown:
87.0% Muslim
11.0% Christian
2.0% Nonreligious

Status of the Church: Freedom of worship; mainly Eastern Orthodox and Roman Catholic

Major Religious Sites: Umayyad Mosque, Chapel of St. Paul, Takieh es Sulaymanieh Mosque, Tomb of Sayyidah Zaynab

Damascus
(duh-**mas**-kuhs)

City Significance/History

Records unearthed in the city indicate that it has been inhabited from the third millennium BC. On the road to Damascus, the apostle Paul was forever changed by his encounter with the Lord Jesus.

Because of its location, the city has been conquered, destroyed, and rebuilt many times. Most of the ancient empires controlled the city during their apex and brought their religion into the city. In the second millennium BC the ancient Arameans built a temple to their god, Hadad, the god of storms and rain. In the first century AD this same temple site was used to construct an enormous temple for the Roman god Jupiter, the god of war, lightning, and thunderbolts. With the rise of Christianity in the Roman Empire in the fourth century, the temple was converted into the Church of St. John the Baptist. It is believed John's head is still at the site.

With Islam's arrival, the church was converted into a mosque, only later to be taken down and rebuilt in the seventh century into the largest mosque of its time. Two of the Umayyad Mosque's minarets are named the Minaret of the Bride and the Minaret of Jesus. Muslim tradition says that Jesus will appear at this location on Judgment Day.

Today Damascus is the commercial and educational center of Syria.

PRAYER POINTS

1. Pray that the many Orthodox and Catholic Christians would be active believers and witnesses.

2. Pray for rural villagers who have moved to slums outside the city because of drought and unemployment. Pray for Christian workers to minister to them.

3. Pray that the Muslim majority would receive godly wisdom from their Christian contacts and that conversions out of Islam would increase. Pray for Christians to have boldness when given the opportunity to witness.

4. Pray for effective evangelism through Christian TV and radio, and for Bibles and Christian literature to have a greater impact.

5. Pray for more full-time workers to serve the churches and to train new leaders in the congregations.

Meaning: "strong, fortified"

Country: Gaza Strip* (undesignated country status)

Population: 410,000

Living Standards: Widespread poverty and malnutrition; over 50% unemployment

Religious Breakdown:
98.7% Muslim
0.7% Christian
0.6% Jewish

Status of the Church: A small persecuted church; mostly Greek Orthodox, some Protestants

Major Religious Sites: Said Hashim Mosque, Umar Mosque, Ibn Uthman Mosque, Church of St. Porphyrius

Gaza
(**gah**-zuh)

City Significance/History

From ancient times Gaza has been ruled by the Egyptians, Philistines, Jews, Arabs, and Turks. Biblically it is known as the city of Samson. The British oversaw it until the Arab–Israeli war of 1948, after which Egypt took control of the area.

In 1967 Israel occupied the Gaza Strip, desiring a buffer zone between them and Egypt. Twenty years later, Palestinian Arabs revolted against Israel's occupation, leading to a period of unrest and violence. In 1993 Palestinians began governing the Gaza Strip and the West Bank, but the permanent status of their rule was not established. In 2000 Israel reoccupied much of the territory.

Attempts to reach an agreement have been thwarted by violence and accusations from both sides. In 2007 the Islamic Resistance Movement, known as Hamas, violently took control of the Gaza Strip. Since then, Israel and Egypt have set up a blockade around the Gazan border.

Life in the Gaza Strip and the city of Gaza is difficult. The economy has suffered greatly because of the blockade. Thousands of buildings have been damaged or destroyed. Many people have suffered the loss of family members to violence, and over half the population are refugees. A small Christian minority exists in this Muslim city.

PRAYER POINTS

1. Pray for the few pastors who live and work in Gaza. With the ongoing violence and religious tension, it is an extremely hard place to minister.

2. Pray that people in Gaza will be able to receive Bibles and Christian literature. Pray that God's Word draws them to him.

3. Pray for a lasting peace agreement and reconciliation between Arabs and Jews.

4. Pray that residents in the Gaza Strip would receive needed food, supplies, and medicine to alleviate their poverty.

5. Pray for protection of believers who are caught in the political crossfire. Pray that they would remain strong in the Lord during hard times.

Meaning: "city of peace"

Country: Israel*

Population: 751,000

Living Standards: Poverty among Palestinians in East Jerusalem

Religious Breakdown:
67.0% Jewish
27.0% Muslim
5.0% Christian
1.0% Other

Status of the Church: Mainly Greek Orthodox and Roman Catholic, some Protestants, a community of Messianic Jews

Major Religious Sites: Western (Wailing) Wall, Temple Mount, Dome of the Rock, Al Aksa Mosque, Church of the Holy Sepulchre

Jerusalem
(jeh-**roo**-suh-lem)

City Significance/History

This holy city is the focal point of the three monotheistic religions—Judaism, Christianity, and Islam. It dates to Abraham's meeting with Melchizedek, the king of Salem, in Genesis 14. Mount Moriah, outside the city, was where Abraham offered his son Isaac on the altar, before God provided the lamb. (Muslims say that it was Ishmael, not Isaac.) Years later, Jesus was crucified outside Jerusalem.

King David built the city as the capital. His son Solomon built the first Jewish temple, later destroyed by the Babylonians in 586 BC. A second temple was built by Zerubbabel and enlarged by Herod the Great. Jesus prophesied its destruction, and in AD 70 the Romans took it apart stone by stone.

Muslims dominated the city for nearly 1,300 years. It is their third holiest city, and the Dome of the Rock was built on the site of the temple mount. The Crusaders briefly ruled during the twelfth century. Mamelukes and Ottomans controlled it until the British occupation during World War I. Jerusalem was reunified again under Israeli rule in 1967.

Religious and political tension between Arabs and Jews has divided the city between East and West Jerusalem. A resolution to each group's claims has not been reached.

PRAYER POINTS

1. Pray that the veil of blindness would be lifted from the Jewish people and that they would see that their own scriptures point to Jesus as the Messiah.

2. Pray that God would bond the Jewish and Arab Christians together in such love that this would point their people to the Messiah.

3. Pray that the spirit of rabbinic Judaism would be bound as the city is perhaps the greatest stronghold of religious spirits in the world.

4. Every year Jews celebrate the Day of Atonement (Yom Kippur). Pray for conviction of sin, repentance, and the spirit of grace and supplication to come upon the people.

5. Pray that both Jews and Muslims living in Jerusalem would realize that Jesus Christ is the only true way to God.

Meaning: "hill of springs"

Country: Israel

Population: 3,256,000

Living Standards: New immigration has stressed the economy

Religious Breakdown:
85.5% Jewish (largely secular)
8.0% Christian
1.5% Muslim
5.0% Other

Status of the Church: Several congregations of Messianic Jews and Arab believers

Major Religious Sites: Tel Aviv — Great Synagogue; Jaffa — Al Mahmudia Mosque, Hassan Bek Mosque, Siksik Mosque

Tel Aviv

(tel-uh-**veev**)

City Significance/History

The seventy kilometers between Jerusalem and Tel Aviv are as different as night and day. The mountains surrounding ancient Jerusalem give way to the Mediterranean coastal plains upon which the modern city of Tel Aviv was built.

In 1909 some sixty Jewish families sought to create a Hebrew city of their own. Just north of Jaffa (Joppa) they bought land and created Tel Aviv. This new city attracted Jewish immigrants from Europe.

Jaffa is where Jonah caught a ship to Tarshish and where Peter had his vision

The 70 km between Jerusalem and Tel Aviv are as different as night and day

regarding the spiritual "cleanness" of the Gentiles. Through this ancient port, now engulfed in the rapid expansion of metropolitan Tel Aviv, passed the timbers used for building the First Temple in Jerusalem.

Tel Aviv was the lifeline for the Jews in Jerusalem during the War of Independence in 1948, and was the capital of the new Israeli state for a brief time. Tel Aviv has become the main center for commerce and business in Israel, and its international airport is the gateway to the country.

PRAYER POINTS

1. Pray for unity among the local leadership as well as between the Arab and Jewish believers. Pray that judgment and criticism in the body of Messiah would be gone.

2. Pray that believers would have greater boldness to witness publicly to residents who are spiritually open.

3. Pray for strategic outreach centers to be established in the city's heart and for more Hebrew-speaking teachers and evangelists.

4. Tel Aviv is the "sin capital" and Jaffa the "drug capital" of Israel. Pray against the remaining Canaanite strongholds of immorality, hedonism, and drugs.

5. The youth are searching for spiritual reality, often through New Age and occult activity. Pray for an effective strategy to reach the city's young people.

Meaning: "in the city"

Country: Turkey

Population: 10,530,000

Living Standards: Swelling population has led to poor areas and shantytowns on outskirts of city

Religious Breakdown:
96.3% Muslim
2.0% Nonreligious
1.4% Christian
0.3% Other

Status of the Church: Seat of the Greek Orthodox Church as well as the Turkish Orthodox and Armenian Churches

Major Religious Sites: Hagia Sophia, Sultan Ahmed (Blue) Mosque, Suleyman Mosque, Eyup Mosque, Topkapi Palace

Istanbul
(is-tan-**bool**)

City Significance/History

Istanbul's strategic location has been important since its beginning. Dorian Greeks led by Byzas started a fishing village here in 657 BC named Byzantium. The city was razed and rebuilt by the Romans in the second century AD. Constantine captured the city in 324 and made Constantinople the "New Rome." The Byzantines ruled their empire from here for the next one thousand years until the Muslim Ottoman Turks captured the city in 1453.

Istanbul is the only city to span two continents, Europe and Asia, with the Bosphorus Strait separating the two. The strait is the gateway between the Mediterranean Sea and the Black Sea.

In 537 Justinian completed the Hagia Sophia, the largest and most beautiful church ever built, standing as a testimony to the Lord Jesus Christ. Like most of the churches in Turkey, it was converted into a mosque. To promote religious harmony in the city, it is now a museum.

Istanbul continues to be a strategic city. Industry, commerce, and a major port enhance its importance. Being the largest city in Turkey, it sets the pace for Westernization. Its population, already the largest in Turkey, is exploding through rural migration.

PRAYER POINTS

1. Pray that God would use the city's ancient roots as a religious and political capital to reach many throughout the Muslim world.

2. Pray for unity and love among the local Turkish fellowships.

3. Pray that the religious freedom in Turkey and openness to new ideas will allow many young people to hear the gospel and turn to Jesus.

4. Pray that the Turkish government will continue to oppose radical Muslim groups and prevent terrorist activities.

5. Pray for the development of Christian radio and TV programming, and for the distribution of Christian videos, especially the *Jesus* film. Pray for more people to use Bible correspondence courses to learn about Jesus.

Meaning: "narrow rocky gorge"

Country: Turkey*

Population: 3,908,000

Living Standards: Slums on outskirts of city

Religious Breakdown:
97.5% Muslim
2.0% Nonreligious
0.2% Christian
0.3% Other

Status of the Church: Several small Turkish fellowships

Major Religious Sites: Haci Bayram Camii (Mosque), Ataturk Mausoleum, Kocatepe Camii, Hisar Citadel, Temple of Augustus (originally a shrine to Cybele)

Ankara
(**ang**-kuh-ruh)

City Significance/History

Throughout its history Ankara has been a fortified trade center in Asia Minor. Located on the east–west and north–south trade routes, Ankara has shaped political and world history. This crossroads location allowed it to grow and influence many other lands because world news and events traveled with the traders. They would tell stories about what was going on in other parts of the world.

Almost every invading military force conquered Ankara. The ancient Hittites lived in Central Anatolia. Later, the crusaders fought for the Hisar Citadel, capturing it only long enough to have the Muslim forces drive them out.

Today Ankara has been restored as a city of great importance and world influence. It is now the home of many government offices, embassies, universities, and medical centers.

Ankara has shaped political and world history

Turkey has an important role in shaping other central Asian Muslim countries because many of the people in these countries share Turkic roots. Turkey began working toward membership in the European Union in 2005.

PRAYER POINTS

1. Pray that the Holy Spirit would strengthen the indigenous Turkish fellowships and that as they are strengthened, they will witness to the Muslim Turks.

2. Pray that new believers will mature spiritually and enter into faithful leadership.

3. Pray that young, single believers will find Christian spouses so that model Christian homes can be established to draw people to Christ.

4. Pray that Christians will find good, steady employment to relieve the economic persecution they suffer as minorities.

5. Pray that the large university student population will be reached with the gospel. Pray for ministries to develop new and innovative ways to do this.

Meaning: "myrrh"

Country: Turkey

Population: 2,724,000

Living Standards: Inflation has stressed the economy

Religious Breakdown:
96.0% Muslim
2.0% Nonreligious
1.7% Christian
0.3% Other

Status of the Church: NATO and expatriate congregations, a small number of Turkish fellowships

Major Religious Sites: Kadifekale (Mt. Pagus), Temple of Artemis (at nearby Ephesus), Sadirvanalti Mosque, Hisar Mosque, Kestane Pazah Mosque, St. Polycarp's Church

Izmir

(iz-**meer**)

City Significance/History

The birthplace of the poet Homer, Izmir (Smyrna until 1923) is considered one of the most beautiful cities on the Mediterranean Sea. Its strategic location has brought many conquerors—Alexander the Great, the Romans, the Byzantines, and the Ottomans.

In 1922, as Ataturk, the founder of the modern Turkish republic, was driving the Greeks out of the city, a disastrous fire broke out and burned most of Smyrna. Until that year there were more Jews and Christians living in the city than Muslims.

A new modern city arose from the

Izmir was the home of an ancient Christian church

ashes, with wide streets and contemporary architecture. Today this predominantly Muslim city is a busy seaport connecting Turkey with Europe and Africa. It is an industrial center and the location of a NATO command center.

Izmir was the home of an ancient Christian church. Smyrna, the former name of Izmir, is one of the seven churches addressed in the book of Revelation. The ruins of the city of Ephesus are nearby. St. Polycarp's Church in Izmir memorializes the martyrdom of the second-century bishop, Polycarp.

PRAYER POINTS

1. Pray that the entrenched greed, materialism, and immorality in the city will be broken by the power of God.

2. Pray that church buildings will be protected meeting places for seekers, and open atmospheres where the gospel can be explained clearly.

3. Pray for students from the two universities to come to Christ and to reach out to fellow students.

4. Pray for more Turkish Christian fellowships to develop in the city, and for faithful leaders, willing to endure persecution, to be raised up to lead the fellowships.

6. Pray that Turkish Christian converts would find strength and encouragement among other believers and that they would lead resistant family members to Christ.

Meaning: "God's gift"

Country: Iraq*

Population: 5,891,000

Living Standards: Buildings and infrastructure damaged by war

Religious Breakdown:
95.0% Muslim
4.2% Christian
0.6% Nonreligious
0.2% Other

Status of the Church: Orthodox and Catholics have ancient roots; a few evangelicals

Major Religious Sites: Marjan Mosque, Kadhimain Mosque

Baghdad
(**bag**-dad)

City Significance/History

After the Flood, the people built an extremely high tower. All the ethnic groups in the world migrated from the Tower of Babel after the confusion of languages. The site later become the city of Babylon, center of the empires of Hammurabi and Nebuchadnezzar. Split in half by the Tigris River, it was world famous for its Hanging Gardens.

Persians, Greeks, and Romans fought for and dominated the area because of the agricultural potential of the fertile Tigris valley. By the ninth century, Baghdad had grown to nearly one million people and was part of the predominately Muslim empire of Adu Jafur al-Mansur. His empire stretched from western China to northern Africa. People traveled to Baghdad because it was the educational center of the known world.

Many other powers controlled the area after al-Mansur's empire lost power and wealth. The city went into economic decline and the population dwindled.

In the 1930s Iraq became an independent country, with Baghdad as the capital. Villagers flocked to the capital to better their lives. The Gulf War and Iraq War inflicted heavy damage on the city, including its power, water, and transportation systems. Many government buildings were bombed.

PRAYER POINTS

1. Pray for an influx of Bibles and Christian literature, and for the Word of God to produce a great harvest.

2. Pray for peace and restoration in this area that has experienced two recent wars. Pray that God would bind spirits of violence and hatred between religious groups.

3. Pray that Shiite and Sunni Muslims will turn from violence toward each other and seek forgiveness. Pray that this would lead them away from their religion to true forgiveness in Christ.

4. The *Jesus* film has been shown on national TV. Pray for its continued showing and distribution, and that a great harvest would result.

5. Pray for revival in the Orthodox and Catholic churches and continued growth in the evangelical house groups.

Meaning: "plain" or "pure, beautiful"

Country: Iran*

Population: 8,221,000

Living Standards: High inflation and unemployment rate; slums in South Tehran

Religious Breakdown:
98.3% Muslim
0.9% Christian
0.3% Baha'i
0.5% Other

Status of the Church: Armenians are the largest group; persecution and limited freedom

Major Religious Sites: Aramgah-e Imam Khomeini (Khomeini's grave), Sepahsalar Mosque, Armenian Cathedral, King's Mosque

Tehran

(teh-**rahn**)

City Significance/History

Located in the foothills of the Alborz Mountains, Tehran was a little village along the trade routes. With time, a fortified city protected the merchants and travelers. In the late twelfth to the seventeenth century, Mongol and Safaid invaders captured and developed the city.

A period of turmoil followed until Agha Muhammad raised an army that conquered the whole of Persia. His capital was Tehran, where he had himself crowned Shah (the monarch of the area). Other shahs took his place as the city continued to develop. Adobe homes were built with little thought to city planning two hundred years ago.

As the twentieth century arrived, so did modernization. The streets followed a grid system, the population expanded (arriving mostly from rural Iran), and pollution become a rising health concern. The Shah was replaced in 1979 by the Ayatollah, and Iran moved from looking to the West to Islamic fundamentalism.

The Iran–Iraq War forced many people living in western Iran to seek jobs and safety in the capital. Tehran continued to grow, with many slum communities filling the southern suburbs. This city, filled with both ancient sites and skyscrapers, is now the most populous in the Middle East and among the twenty most populous cities in the world.

PRAYER POINTS

1. Christian leaders have been martyred and other Christians have been imprisoned. Pray that government persecution of the church will end.

2. Pray for the believers to remain bold and full of joy, and that constitutional freedoms will be restored as they face increased opposition from the Muslim majority.

3. Pray that this center of Islamic fundamentalism would no longer export its tyranny to other Muslim countries.

4. Pray that missionaries would again be allowed to work in Iran, especially among the younger generation, which is open to new ideas.

5. Pray for the Holy Spirit to renew the traditional Armenian and Nestorian (Assyrian) Christian communities.

Meaning: "place of martyrdom"
Country: Iran
Population: 2,654,000
Living Standards: Migration has increased the number of poor communities
Religious Breakdown:
99.0% Muslim
0.3% Baha'i
0.2% Christian
0.5% Other
Status of the Church: Very few churches; persecution and limited freedom
Major Religious Sites: Imam Reza Shrine Complex, Gombade Sabz Mausoleum, Khwajeh Rabil Mausoleum

Mashhad
(muh-**shad**)

City Significance/History

Mashhad is Iran's holiest city. In the ninth century, Imam Reza (the only official imam buried in Iran until Ayatollah Khomeini) was poisoned and martyred in the city. He was the eighth imam (head spiritual leader) of Shiite Islam. His holy position made his tomb a sacred place for pilgrims to worship.

Before Imam Reza died, the city was known as Sanabad, a small village in the north of Persia. After his death, pilgrims came and ended up staying in Mashhad. The village grew into a small city because of his shrine. Sunni Muslim forces sacked the city, followed by the Mongols in the thirteenth century.

The shrine was badly damaged and, after time, rebuilt.

In the sixteenth century, three Safavid dynasty rulers established Shiite Islam for the whole territory. The shrine was restored and enlarged, and a mosque was built. These rulers made pilgrimages to the site, and since then it has become the most holy Shiite pilgrimage site in Iran. Every year millions of people visit the shrine.

Mashhad, Iran's second largest city, is located in the northeast near the border of Turkmenistan. A railroad built in 1996 links the city to Turkmenistan and the rest of central Asia.

PRAYER POINTS

1. Pray that this Islamic stronghold would be penetrated by the transforming power of the gospel.

2. Pray that Christian radio and videos would be widely received and distributed.

3. Pray that Bibles and Christian literature sent through the mail would reach their destinations.

4. Terrorist acts at religious sites have claimed the lives of many pilgrims. Pray that disillusionment would cause seekers to find Jesus.

5. Pray for strength and joy for the believers living in such a hostile environment. Pray for the growth of their fellowships.

CENTRAL ASIA

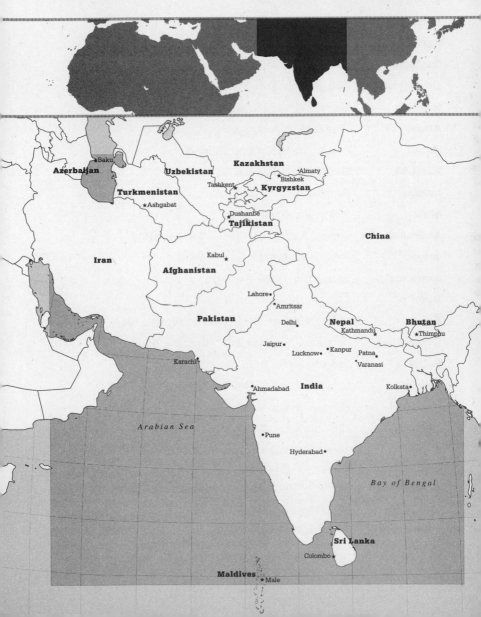

Azerbaijan
★Baku

Turkmenistan
★Ashgabat

Uzbekistan
Tashkent

Kazakhstan
★Almaty
★Bishkek
Kyrgyzstan

Dushanbe
Tajikistan

China

Iran

Kabul ★
Afghanistan

Lahore•
•Amritsar

Pakistan
Delhi•

Nepal
Kathmandu

Bhutan
★Thimphu

Jaipur•
Lucknow• •Kanpur Patna•
•Varanasi

Karachi•

•Ahmadabad   India   Kolkata•

Arabian Sea

•Pune

Hyderabad•

Bay of Bengal

Sri Lanka
Colombo ★

Maldives
★Male

CENTRAL ASIA
MAJOR UNREACHED PEOPLES

City	Peoples
Baku	Azeri, Tatar, Bashkir, Chechen
Ashgabat	Turkmen, Uzbek, Russian, Kazakh
Tashkent	Uzbek, Tajik, Kazakh, Russian
Dushanbe	Tajik, Uzbek, Korean
Bishkek	Kyrgyz, Uzbek, Russian, Ukrainian
Almaty	Kazakh, Uzbek, Tatar, Russian, Uygur
Kabul	Pushto, Hazara, Tajik, Turkmen
Karachi	Sindhi, Punjabi, Pushtun, Baloch
Lahore	Punjabi, Urdu, Hazara, Tajik
Male	Maldivian, Sinhalese
Ahmadabad	Central Bhil, Mina, Sindhi, Southern Bhil
Jaipur	Rajasthani, Bangri, Bagri, Wagdi
Amritsar	Sikh, Mina, Urdu, Garhwali
Delhi	Urdu, Kashmiri, Sikh, Mina
Pune	Magadhi Bihari, Berar Marathi, Konkanese
Hyderabad	Deccanni, Bundelkhandi, Gormati, Tulu
Kolkata	Bengali, Hindi, Urdu, Nepali
Kanpur	Awadhi, Bihari, Urdu, Garhwali
Varanasi	Bhojpuri Bihar, Malvi, Maitili
Lucknow	Bhojpuri Bihar, Kanauji, Urdu, Garhwali
Patna	Bhojpuri Bihari, Chattisgarhi, Kortha Bihari, Nagpuri Bihari
Kathmandu	Tibeto-Burma, Nepalese, Maitili, Bhojpuri Bihari
Thimphu	Bhutanese, Drukpa, Nepali
Colombo	Ceylon Moor, Sinhalese, Tamil

Meaning: "violent winds"
Country: Azerbaijan*
Population: 1,931,000
Living Standards: Economic growth due to oil exports; 250,000 refugees and internally displaced people; severe air pollution
Religious Breakdown:
83.0% Muslim
8.6% Christian
8.0% Nonreligious
0.4% Other
Status of the Church: Russian Orthodox, Armenian, and Molokan
Major Religious Sites: Lezgi Mosque, Dzhuma Mosque, Adjarbek Mosque, Synyk Kala Minaret

Baku
(bah-**koo**)

City Significance/History

Oil pools allowed people to scoop oil out of the ground and worship their god. A perpetual fire was tended by the priests. The Zoroastrians believed in Ahura Mazda, the one God who would send his son as a special "expression" of himself to the lower world. It was believed a virgin would bathe in a lake in the east, become pregnant, and give birth to a son.

Baku, a fortified township, rose and fell as different powers marched through the area. The Persians, Muslims, Arabs, Seljuk Turks, Mongols, and Russians all had control over this low-lying city on the Caspian Sea.

Oil, just below the surface, attracted many into the area. By 1901 Baku supplied a little over half of the world's oil. During World Wars I and II, Baku became an object of military importance. Hitler sent troops to conquer the oil fields, but the Russians held them off at Stalingrad.

In 1990 Baku was the location of intense fighting between Soviet and rebel forces. In 1991 Azerbaijan declared independence from the USSR, which collapsed the same year.

After seventy years as Soviet republic, Azerbaijan now looks to their Muslim neighbors to the south for trade and economic assistance. Baku is considered a center of Islamic culture.

PRAYER POINTS

1. Nationalistic hopes have fanned an Islamic revival. Pray that freedom of religion will continue and anti-Christian sentiment will diminish.

2. Pray that the youth of the city might hear the gospel and be saved.

3. There are no Azerbaijani congregations. Pray that God will establish an indigenous church and raise up its leaders.

4. Pray that skilled tentmakers will be called to work in the city.

5. The oil fields and wells have caused great pollution. Pray for the people suffering because of polluted water, air, and land.

Meaning: "city in love"

Country: Turkmenistan*

Population: 892,000

Living Standards: Many new buildings, but widespread poverty among the people

Religious Breakdown:
86.0% Muslim
9.9% Nonreligious
4.0% Christian
0.1% Other

Status of the Church: Russian Orthodox, Baptist, and charismatic churches; only a few Turkmen believers

Major Religious Sites: Behaist's Mosque, Kan Abdul Qasim-Babir Mosque (nearby Anau)

Ashgabat
(**ahsh**-guh-baht)

City Significance/History

The name of the city comes from the tale of two lovers who made Allah mad. Allah turned the woman into a river and the man into a city. A desert was placed between them to separate them.

The Kara-Kum Desert, with its scorching heat, made nomadic life difficult. Water could only be found in a few oasis towns scattered across the desert. At the Kopet Dag Oasis in the nineteenth century, the Russians built a stronghold for their trade interests in Persia. They constructed railways across the desert, causing Ashgabat to become a growing north–south trade center.

In 1948 an earthquake measuring 9.0 on the Richter scale shook apart the mud brick homes, leaving only twelve buildings standing and over one hundred thousand people dead. From the rubble sprang a new and reinforced concrete city.

With construction of the Kara-Kum Canal, which allows water to flow from the Caspian Sea into the desert, Ashgabat has a large water source that enables large agricultural projects to develop.

This capital city is famous worldwide for its handmade carpets.

PRAYER POINTS

1. The eldest men in Turkmen society are respected by family and friends. Pray that God will touch these men and that they in turn will spread knowledge of Christ, family to family.

2. Islamic and Turkmen culture had long been suppressed by the Soviets, and now many are seeking spiritual things. Pray that the search will show them their need for a Savior.

3. Ashgabat is home to many educated people who are open to new ideas. Pray for these people to seize opportunities to listen to the gospel.

4. Pray that God will stir an interest in the Russian scriptures available among the Turkmen. Many Turkmen read Russian and can learn about Jesus in the Word. Pray for the translation of the Bible into Turkmen to be completed and effective.

5. Pray for workers to equip the indigenous church.

Meaning: "city of stone"
Country: Uzbekistan*
Population: 2,247,000
Living Standards: Increased poverty since the fall of communism
Religious Breakdown:
  82.4% Muslim
  14.0% Nonreligious
  3.0% Christian
  0.6% Other
Status of the Church: Russian and Korean congregations; a few Uzbek believers
Major Religious Sites: Barak Khana Mosque and Madrassa, Sheik Zein-ad-Din Mausoleum, Rakat (New) Mosque

Tashkent
(tash-**kent**)

City Significance/History

The fourth largest city of the former Soviet Union and the first city of Central Asia, Tashkent sits as a monument to the current century in a land of ancient and, in many ways, unchanged peoples.

Almost completely destroyed by an earthquake in 1966, Soviet planners rebuilt Tashkent like a typical Russian city—with tall office buildings, numerous parks, an ornate subway system, and tree-lined boulevards. The decisions made in Tashkent, the capital of Uzbekistan, influence the entire region.

Before the fall of the Soviet Union in 1991, Uzbeks born and raised in Tashkent often were more comfortable speaking Russian than the Uzbek of their grandparents. Uzbek, now the official language, has forced many Russian-speaking but otherwise competent professionals to leave the country. With the new currency (the som) and the economy rapidly moving toward hyperinflation, some people started seeking economic salvation in emigration to the West.

In an attempt to hinder the church, local Muslims petitioned the government to force the Protestant churches to stop evangelizing Uzbeks in 1994, although the constitution upholds freedom of religion. None of the Christian church representatives signed this agreement.

PRAYER POINTS

1. Pray for believers as they face increasing pressure and persecution—for boldness, wisdom, unity, and love.

2. Praise God for what he is doing among the Uzbeks and other nationalities in Tashkent. Ask him to send more laborers into the harvest fields.

3. Pray for wisdom for the president and his cabinet, and that justice and righteousness might reign in their hearts and in their decrees.

4. Because Tashkent is the Islamic capital of Central Asia, all of the surrounding Muslim republics look to the *muftis* (Islamic scholars) based here. Pray for a dissatisfaction with Islam and an openness to Christianity.

5. Pray for the few Uzbek believers—that a truly indigenous church would develop.

Meaning: "second night" or "Monday"

Country: Tajikistan*

Population: 689,000

Living Standards: Widespread unemployment and poverty

Religious Breakdown:
83.0% Muslim
13.7% Nonreligious
3.0% Christian
0.3% Other

Status of the Church: Russian and Ukrainian churches, a few national believers

Major Religious Sites: Adjnatepe Hill (Buddhist), Shamaisur Mosque, Khaji Yakub Mosque, Yakub Charkhi Tomb

Dushanbe

(do-**sham**-buh)

City Significance/History

The Silk Road twisted its way along the foothills and steppes of the Pamirs. A mud fortress in the Gissar Valley rested next to the Dushanbinka River. Buddhist traders followed the trade routes from India into Central Asia, bringing Buddhism with them. The local people in the seventh century built a twelve-meter-high Buddha as a shrine to worship.

Muslim invaders pushed in from the south to be replaced by others invading from the north. The small city was of little interest and remained poor until the Russians invaded and made the city the capital of the Tajik Republic. A railway was built connecting it with the greater Soviet Union, which brought Russians to the city to establish it as Stalinabad. The name was later changed back to Dushanbe. The city grew in population as industries were established. With the collapse of the USSR came the collapse of peace in Dushanbe.

A civil war lasted from 1992 until 1997, during which time Islamists, nationalists, and democratic reformists sought to overthrow the old Russian-backed government. Tens thousands of people were killed, and Dushanbe was badly damaged. With a peace agreement in place, many new buildings have been constructed.

PRAYER POINTS

1. Pray that the leaders will bring continued peace to this city and that they will discover the true Prince of Peace.

2. Many Russian, Ukrainian, and German Christians emigrated because of the civil war. Pray for new growth and revival of the church.

3. Pray that Muslim Tajik will turn to the Lord and that workers fluent in the language will be raised up.

4. Pray for the dissemination of the Tajik Bible and the *Jesus* film.

5. Pray that the few Tajik believers would reach out to their fellow Tajiks with love and boldness.

Meaning: "A stick used to whip mare's milk"

Country: Kyrgyzstan*

Population: 869,000

Living Standards: Most modernized city in poor country

Religious Breakdown:
68.0% Muslim
23.4% Nonreligious
7.6% Christian
1.0% Other

Status of the Church: Mainly Russian and Ukrainian Orthodox; some German Protestants

Major Religious Sites: Gogol Street Mosque

Bishkek

(bish-**kek**)

City Significance/History

The massive Tien Shan mountains separate western China from the steppes of Central Asia. The nomadic Kirghiz (or Kyrgyz) living in round *yurts* (tents) would move seasonally with their herds from the mountains to the flatlands. The mountains forced the trade routes to pass along the foothills, and many people desired to control these routes. The Chinese, other Central Asians, Arabs, and Mongols would storm the region seeking control. For most of the past two millennia, others have ruled the land.

Bishkek, also known as Frunze, was one of many settlements established along the long Silk Road. From these sites, travelers would journey along the trade route, and local peoples would buy and sell goods. One khan would gain control, only to be replaced by another in the continual struggle to control this strategic site.

In 1825 a fortress was built along the Chu River Valley to protect tax collectors from the Kirghiz Silk Road pirates. The Russians later invaded Central Asia, and this small Silk Road fortification was easy prey for them in 1865. Russia established a stronghold and city. While under Soviet control, the area developed as a educational and economic center. Kyrgyzstan gained independence in 1991 with Bishkek as its capital.

PRAYER POINTS

1. Pray that the residual occultism, shamanism, and demonic possession in the culture will be broken.

2. Pray for unity among the immigrant, ethnic Christians. Their divisions have negatively impacted the church's witness.

3. Pray for the developing Kyrgyz church, that it would be truly indigenous and led by godly leaders.

4. Pray that outside workers would use wisdom and discernment in sharing the gospel within a context sensitive to Kyrgyz culture.

5. Pray for the distribution of the Kyrgyz New Testament and other Christian media and literature.

Meaning: "father of apples"
Country: Kazakhstan
Population: 1,240,000
Living Standards: Economic growth and increased wealth
Religious Breakdown:
  41.6% Muslim
  30.0% Nonreligious
  28.0% Christian
  0.4% Other
Status of the Church: Russian Orthodox Church, sixty Kazakh churches
Major Religious Sites: Pushkin Street Mosque

Almaty
(al-**mah**-tee)

City Significance/History

Kazakhs take pride in Almaty, the largest city in Kazakhstan, known for its beautiful setting against the Tien Shan mountains. The Silk Road passed through the area, bringing the Mongol hordes from the north, who left their Mongol features and the Muslim religion.

Today Almaty is the business, historical, and educational center of the country. To prevent the disintegration of the country, the Parliament voted to move the capital from Almaty to the northern city of Astana in 1997. The fall of Communism toppled both religious and political structures, forcing Kazakhs into an ideological vacuum. Having always been told what to do and believe, Kazakhs now have freedom to choose. Islam attracts some because it provides clear directives on life and supports Kazakh heritage. Other religions and cults are clamoring for allegiance, while secular materialism is successfully winning many hearts. Although there are areas of poverty on the city's outskirts, central Almaty is a place of visible wealth.

Historically, ethnic Russians have been part of the Orthodox Church, but more and more people are turning to evangelicalism. This has caused cultural tension, and some churches have experienced government censoring and persecution.

PRAYER POINTS

1. Pray that the communist forces of atheism would be completely eliminated, and pray that this ideological vacuum will be filled with Christian belief. Pray against the spread of false religions that seek to trap Kazakhs.

2. Many Islamic nations are trying to influence Kazakhstan, and pressure to restrict Christian witness is growing. Pray that the gospel would not be restricted.

3. Pray that Almaty would be a hub where visiting Kazakh leaders, students, and businessmen would find the Lord and then spread his light throughout Kazakhstan.

4. Pray that people would realize the emptiness of materialism and instead pursue things that have eternal value.

5. Pray that the entire Bible will be translated into Kazakh and distributed widely.

Meaning: "straw bridge" or "Cain"
Country: Afghanistan*
Population: 3,768,000
Living Standards: Widespread poverty, conditions improving since 2001
Religious Breakdown:
99.7% Muslim
0.2% Christian
0.1% Other
Status of the Church: Only a handful of secret believers
Major Religious Sites: Shire of Ali, Khair Khaneh Temple, Asmayi Temple (Hindu), Poli Khishti Mosque, Pious Martyr's Cemetery

Kabul
(**kah**-buhl)

City Significance/History

The memoirs of Babur the Great say Cain built Kabul. Located on a 5,000-foot-high basin surrounded by mountains, Kabul developed as a trade center. People would sift the sand of Kabul River seeking gold dust. Surya, a sun god, was worshiped with blood sacrifices. The central Asmayi mountain is named after an eight-armed Hindu goddess of nature, whose shrine lies at one of the gates of the city.

Kabul has been repeatedly conquered by invading armies such as the Greeks, Mongols, Arabs, English, and Soviets. The Kabul wall was breached by Muslims in the seventh century after resisting for one hundred years.

In 1978 a Communist coup set the stage for the Soviet invasion a year and a half later. The ensuing war left 80 percent of the villages destroyed. During the eight-year Soviet occupation, Kabul was protected from destruction. When Najibullah's puppet regime fell, the victorious *mujahidin* factions turned on each other and largely destroyed the city.

In 1996 the Taliban siezed control of the city and imposed strict Islamic rule. They were overthrown in 2001 when the U.S. military intervened and bombed the city. Since then, many refugees have returned to the city. With the collapse of the rural economy, many rural Afghanis have also come to the city.

PRAYER POINTS

1. Even though the Taliban was overthrown in 2001, there remains little religious freedom in Afghanistan. Pray for increased freedom for all people to practice their faith and for Christian missionaries to be able to safely minister here.

2. The country is in need of a strong leader. Pray that a godly leader like King Cyrus would be raised up to establish just laws and order in the city.

3. Pray for continued peace in a city that has been ravaged by warring factions. Pray that terrorist groups like the Taliban will not regain control of the area.

4. Pray that God would use difficult times to draw people to himself and advance his gospel. Pray also for the complete reconstruction of the city.

5. Pray that a viable fellowship of indigenous believers will be raised up in the city.

Meaning: original name "Kullachi"
Country: Pakistan
Population: 13,052,000
Living Standards: Many refugees, slums in parts of the city
Religious Breakdown:
94.9% Muslim
3.3% Christian
1.5% Hindu
0.3% Other
Status of the Church: Roman Catholic and Protestant churches
Major Religious Sites: Quaid-i-Azam Mausoleum, Defense Society Mosque, Abdullah Shah Ghazi Shrine (Sufi)

Karachi
(kuh-**rah**-chee)

City Significance/History

Until the mid-nineteenth century, Karachi was only a small fishing village and fort wedged between the Arabian Sea and the expanse of desert to the north. At the time the British were gaining interest in the area. They built a naval base and moved the territorial capital from Hyderabad to Karachi.

Railways connecting Karachi with the north were built, the port expanded, roads were paved, and the city became a place of migration for the first time. The population grew quickly. As the capital and commercial center, many people relocated to the area after massive irrigation projects turned the hot, dry desert into farm land.

In 1963 the capital of Pakistan was moved to the planned city of Islamabad. Karachi, the main port city for the country, continued to be the commercial center. Islamabad is conservative, with many women in veils and traditional black garb. Karachi, in contrast, has Western dress and is more liberal.

Karachi's most impressive monument is the tomb of Muhammad Ali Jinnah, the man who led the country to independence and served as the first governor general.

Karachi has Western dress and is more liberal

PRAYER POINTS

1. Pray for effective ministry to the one million or more drug addicts in the city.

2. Pray for evangelization of the Mohajirs, Ismaili Muslims, and Afghan refugees.

3. Pray for the salvation of one million Balochs in the city; there are few known Baloch believers in the world.

4. Pray that interethnic conflicts, kidnappings, and violent crimes in the city will cause people to look to Jesus for answers. Pray for Christians who are targets of violence.

5. Pray that the few Pushtu-speaking believers can boldly declare the gospel to the two million Pukhtun people in the city.

6. Pray that the church would be healed of divisions and delivered of Hindu superstitions and occultic practices, and that pastors would be strengthened.

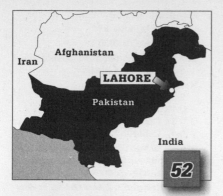

Meaning: "iron," suggesting fortification

Country: Pakistan, Punjab Province*

Population: 7,092,000

Living Standards: Population growth has stressed water infrastructure

Religious Breakdown:
94.1% Muslim
5.1% Christian
0.5% Hindu
0.3% Other

Status of the Church: Roman Catholic and Protestant churches

Major Religious Sites: Sunehri Mosque, Badshahi Mosque, Wazir Khan Mosque, Data Ganj Bakhsh Hajveri Mausoleum, Masjid-e-Shuhuda

Lahore
(luh-**hor**)

City Significance/History

Built on the trade routes between the Indian subcontinent and Central Asia, Lahore has seen many battles. Invading forces have repeatedly fought over the city, which has been the capital of Punjab for over a thousand years. The Ravi River provides all the water needed for its hot, arid environment. A massive canal was built for irrigation, allowing the city to spread out along its banks.

In the eleventh century Islamic forces took control of the city. Muslim factions battled for it over the following centuries. The Moghul rulers in the sixteenth century made it into an Islamic center for learning and the arts. The walled Lahore Fort, built in 1560, became the city's main defense. Its repeated destruction and rebuilding testifies to the city as a battleground. In 1770 Lahore was sold to a Hindu Sikh ruler, and later the British took control. With the independence of Pakistan in 1947, the city returned to Islamic leadership.

Karachi is the commercial center, Islamabad is the political center, and Lahore is the cultural center of Pakistan. As the cultural center, it is the protector of Islamic ways and traditions. The Shalimar Garden, built by Shah Jahan in 1642, is a popular place for escaping the extremely hot summer months.

PRAYER POINTS

1. Pray that those who practice folk Islam, worshiping the city's patron saint, would hear the good news of Jesus Christ.

2. Pray for the protection of new believers who undergo persecution mainly by relatives.

3. Pray that backbiting, politics, and corruption would no longer hinder the church's witness and that harmony, purity, and unity would instead characterize the church. Pray for church leaders to lead the way in this.

4. Pray that the provincial assembly in Lahore would have God-fearing representatives making godly decisions for the welfare of the province and country.

5. A number of Christian organizations have their headquarters in the city. Pray for wisdom for their leaders and for effectiveness in their ministry.

Meaning: "mountain"
Country: Maldives*
Population: 104,000
Living Standards: Most people live at subsistence levels
Religious Breakdown:
98.6% Muslim
0.7% Buddhist
0.3% Christian
0.4% Other
Status of the Church: No officially recognized Maldivian believers; no non-Muslim places of worship
Major Religious Sites: Grand Friday Mosque, Hukuru Mosque

Male
(**mah**-lee)

City Significance/History

Little is known about the ancient history of Male. It is believed that the small island nation of the Maldives was founded by sailors from India, Sri Lanka, and other countries. Most of the 1,192 islands are only a meter or two above sea level.

Islam is the only religion

It is likely that the people worshiped the sun as their god, with beliefs also in evil spirits. Ancient temple sites have been converted into mosques. Most mosques in the world are built with their main wall facing Mecca; in the Maldives, when the Muslims pray, they face the corner of the mosque because the old foundations face the sun.

Islam entered the country in the twelfth century when Arab and North African merchants established control. By the sixteenth century the Portuguese desired more influence in the East Indian trade and built a fort at Male. They replaced the existing Muslim sultan and expanded their dominance. The sultan's followers rebelled and massacred the Portuguese.

The sultan firmly established Islam as the state religion, and Islam has continued to be the only religion of the area. Male has been protected by other rulers but never completely controlled by outside powers.

PRAYER POINTS

1. Pray that Bibles and Christian literature may be legally imported, and that examination of incoming mail will end.

2. Pray that Bibles in the Dhivehi script will become available and that anti-conversion laws will be changed.

3. Pray that the suspicion of and prejudice against Christianity might be removed.

4. Pray that restrictions against Christian media might be lifted and that the gospel may be heard. Pray that Christian radio programming will be developed.

5. Pray that tentmakers will be able to obtain residency visas to work in the city.

6. Pray that Christian expatriates will have wisdom and discernment when and how they should share the gospel with the city's residents.

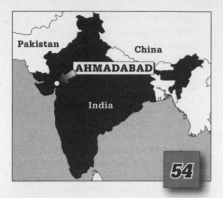

Meaning: "Ahmed's town"

Country: India, Gujarat State

Population: 5,726,000

Living Standards: Growing industry, many slums

Religious Breakdown:
76.0% Hindu
12.0% Muslim
5.0% Sikh
1.6% Christian
5.4% Other

Status of the Church: Various denominations

Major Religious Sites: Jami Masjid Mosque, Sidi Saiyad Mosque, Ahmed Shah Mosque, Hathee Singh Temple

Ahmadabad
(**ah**-muh-duh-bahd)

City Significance/History

Ahmad Shah I, sultan of the Gujarat state of western India, founded the city early in the fifteenth century. The people of the area found life along the Sabarmati River, and there the Shah built the city on the site of Karnavati. Karna was a Hindu god, the son of the Sun and Pritha. It was said that Karna was born clothed with arms and armor. He was later killed in a battle, and his religious fame died with him.

With the city's name change also came a strengthening of Islam. Mosques were built, and Islam grew stronger. The Jami Masjid Mosque was constructed from the demolished Jain Temple. Tensions between Hindus and Muslims continue.

Mahatma Gandhi longed for a peaceful unification of the two religions. From Ahmadabad he walked to the Indian Ocean in protest of the Salt Laws. However, the rise of the BJP, a radical Hindu political party, has threatened to destabilize the country's political life and social balance. The BJP is threatening the freedom of minority religions.

The city is one of India's most important textile centers. Yet it has a huge slum population, which possesses inadequate civil amenities. Many people are illiterate and unemployed, and street children are the by-product of this tragic situation.

PRAYER POINTS

1. The Hindu Navariati festival has also attracted many Christians, adversely affecting their faith. Pray that believers would be renewed by the Holy Spirit.

2. Pray that Christians would reach out to those living in slums. Pray that they can meet both physical and spiritual needs.

3. The city is a stronghold of the BJP. Pray that this radical Hindu party would lose its political influence and stop its opposition to Christianity.

4. Pray for outreaches to the city's two universities. Pray for young Christians to be bold witnesses for Christ.

5. Pray that the government will continue to allow religious freedom and will oppose those who persecute people of other faiths.

Pakistan

China

JAIPUR

India

55

Meaning: "city of victory"

Country: India, Rajasthan State*

Population: 3,136,000

Living Standards: Improving infrastructure, many slums

Religious Breakdown:
89.0% Hindu
8.0% Muslim
0.4% Christian
2.6% Other

Status of the Church: Various denominations, half of the Christians are from South India

Major Religious Sites: Iswari Minar Swarga Sul, Jantar Mantar Observatory

Jaipur
(**jai**-poor)

City Significance/History

Three ancient forts rest on the hills overlooking most of present-day Jaipur. Well water allowed this desert oasis to grow on a dried lake bed. The Amber Fort was the capital of the Mina tribe, who were the original inhabitants. The Jaigarh Fort, containing India's largest cannon, was so impregnable that no enemy breached its walls.

In 1727 Maharaja Jai Singh II planned the expansion of the forts to one large fortified city. The city expanded, and a wall was built around it with seven gates. At night the city gates were closed for protection. On the outside of the gates, long anti-elephant spikes

were mounted to keep enemies from using their elephants to ram the gates.

The color pink was said to be the color of hospitality. When Britain's Prince Albert visited the city in 1883, all the main buildings were painted pink to welcome him. As the provincial capital, Jaipur has continued to keep its traditional pink color.

The wall has been torn down and used to build homes, yet the gates remain. The wall's foundation marks the old city, but Jaipur has expanded outside the old walls. Camels still pull carts down the street as Jaipur keeps its old and new moving together.

PRAYER POINTS

1. Pray that the Muslim Meo people might become responsive to the gospel. Among the Muslim Meo people are no known Christians.

2. The higher caste Hindus (the Rajputs, Jats, and Marwari) have shown little interest in the gospel. Pray that the spiritual powers keeping them in darkness will be broken.

3. Pray for increased conversions through literature distribution, radio evangelism, and Bible correspondence courses, and that churches would multiply.

4. Worship of rats produces conditions that foster pneumonic plague. Pray that the idolatry underlying this health hazard would be bound.

5. The average age at marriage for girls in Rajasthan is fifteen, even though the legal age is eighteen. Pray that laws abolishing child marriages would be obeyed.

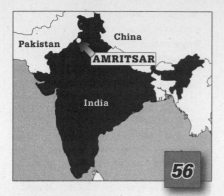

Meaning: "pool of immortality"

Country: India, Punjab State

Population: 1,299,000

Living Standards: Slums on city outskirts

Religious Breakdown:
60.7% Sikh
36.9% Hindu
1.1% Muslim
0.7% Christian
0.6% Other

Status of the Church: Roman Catholics make up the majority; a few evangelicals

Major Religious Sites: The Golden Temple, Durgiana Temple (Hindu)

Amritsar

(uhm-**rit**-ser)

City Significance/History

Hinduism has been in India for thousands of years. Islam entered in the twelfth century, converting many in the north. Violence between the groups has been widespread ever since. In an attempt to unify the two religions, a new religion, Sikhism, was started in the fifteenth century by Guru Nanak. One hundred years later, the fourth Sikh guru founded Amritsar as a holy Sikh city. It quickly became the center of the Sikh religion.

A temple built next to the pool of nectar was destroyed by the Mongol invaders and later rebuilt, this time coated with copper. This Golden Temple is the holiest of all Sikh temples.

When Gandhi was seeking the peaceful withdrawal of the British, Amritsar became the site of one of the largest Indian massacres. The British, trying to establish control in Punjab, opened fire on the Indians. In an attempt to survive the bullets, many Indians jumped into the city's main well. The British killed or wounded over two thousand Indians.

Violence has occurred in the city even after India's independence. In 1984 the Indian army fought against Sikh extremists who had taken the Golden Temple as a fortress. The army stormed the temple, killing upwards of eight hundred civilians and militants. Some two hundred soldiers were also killed.

PRAYER POINTS

1. The Christians are underprivileged, generally nominal, and discouraged. Pray that the Holy Spirit would renew and refresh the believers.

2. Pray that Amritsar will be a city of peace, not violence and killing. Pray that Sikh extremists and others in the city would open their hearts to the gospel.

3. Many caste groups as well as tribal groups are unevangelized. Pray for workers to take the good news of Jesus to these people.

4. Pray that pilgrims to the Golden Temple would instead find the true way to God, the Lord Jesus.

5. The Sikh holy scripture, the Granth Sahib, is located in the Golden Temple. Pray that its influence would be replaced by God's Word.

Meaning: "threshold"
Country: India*
Population: 17,015,000
Living Standards: Four million people live in slum colonies
Religious Breakdown:
52.0% Hindu
25.0% Muslim
20.0% Sikh
3.0% Christian
Status of the Church: Roman Catholic and Protestant congregations
Major Religious Sites: Jama Masjid Mosque, Lakshmi Narayan Temple, Might of Islam Mosque, Nizam-ud-din Shrine

Delhi
(**deh**-lee)

City Significance/History

Delhi has been a hub of activity since the fourth century BC. Traders would come and go to the old city. In the twelfth century Delhi became the capital of Muslim India. The Mogul invaders brought bloodshed and Islam with great force. The Red Fort was built to protect the city and to display the glory of the Mogul Empire.

The capital moved between a number of cities until the British built New Delhi, which remains India's capital today. Old and New Delhi are a mixture of culture, style, and history.

Delhi displays the diversity and contrasts of a Third World urban center in the process of modernization. Imported cars and colorful city buses share the streets with horse-drawn carts and wandering cows. People of varying languages, educational levels, and cultures migrate here from all over India. They are drawn by the economic and educational opportunities. Temples of all shapes and sizes, scattered steeples of ancient churches, and a myriad of mosque minarets reflect the religious diversity.

The capital has mushroomed in size since the British left. Air pollution, high electricity usage, and water shortages have become growing problems, and there is a growing divide between the rich and poor.

PRAYER POINTS

1. Pray that peace and love would replace the spirit of violence and anger in the city.

2. Pray that God would use the government in Delhi to allow more freedom for Christian witness throughout all of India.

3. Little outreach is focused on the Hindus, Muslims, and Sikhs. Pray for workers to be raised up to plant churches among each of these groups.

4. Modernization has strained the city to the limit, with vehicle pollution overwhelming everyone. Pray that the growing disillusionment will turn people to Jesus.

5. Pray for aid and outreach to the four million people who live in the growing slums.

6. The headquarters of many Christian organizations are here. Pray for wisdom for the leaders so that spiritual blessings might flow throughout the country.

Pakistan   China

India

PUNE

58

Meaning: "city of merit"

Country: India, Maharashtra State

Population: 5,010,000

Living Standards: Industry and education center, growing slums due to migration

Religious Breakdown:
80.4% Hindu
10.0% Muslim
4.0% Christian
5.6% Other

Status of the Church: Roman Catholic and Protestant churches

Major Religious Sites: Mahadji Mausoleum, Qamar Ali Darvesh Mosque, Pateleshwar Temple, Parvati Temple, Shinde Chhatri Temple, Saras Buag Ganesh Temple

Pune
(**poo**-nuh)

City Significance/History

Shiva is one of the main gods of Hinduism. For those in the Shaiva tradition, Shiva is the supreme god; there is no other. He is the power of opposites — he is the creator and destroyer, he controls good and evil, he is rest and ceaseless activity.

Shivaji, a great Hindu political leader in the seventeenth century, derived his name from Shiva. Shivaji was born in Pune and led battles against the Muslim Moguls. From Pune, once the capital of the Hindu Maratha Empire, many Hindu social reform movements were launched against the Muslim powers. In the eighteenth century, a temple to Shiva was built as a stronghold of Hinduism.

The British captured the city in the early nineteenth century and turned it into a place to retreat during the monsoons and heat of Bombay. They developed the city into an educational and cultural center, "the Oxford of India." The city has continued to develop as a center for information technology.

Bhagwan Rajneesh, later called Osho, set up an ashram in Pune in the 1970s. After a period of living abroad (he was forced to leave the United States in 1985 because of immigration fraud), he returned to Pune, where he continued to teach a progressive Hinduism. The Osho International Meditation Resort in Pune is a much-visited spiritual center.

PRAYER POINTS

1. Pray for unity among the small Protestant community, particularly that all would be united by a personal and active faith in Jesus Christ.

2. Pray for spiritual renewal among the large minority of Catholics, and pray for growth and outreach in the few evangelical churches.

3. Pray for ministry among the high population of Jains who are largely unevangelized.

4. Shiva grips the hearts of the Hindus living in the area. Pray that Hindus would turn to the loving Father.

5. Pray that Western pilgrims visiting the Osho resort would find the living Lord.

6. This educational center attracts many foreign students, mainly African. Pray for workers and outreaches to the universities.

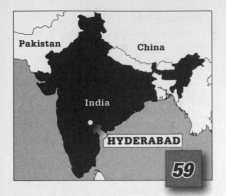

Meaning: "lion town"

Country: India, Andhra Pradesh State*

Population: 6,761,000

Living Standards: Two million people live in slums

Religious Breakdown:
85.5% Hindu
8.5% Muslim
4.3% Christian
1.7% Other

Status of the Church: Many churches of different denominations

Major Religious Sites: Birla Mandir Hindu Temple, Mecca Masjid Mosque, Charminar Mosque, Mahankali Temple

Hyderabad
(**hai**-der-uh-bad)

City Significance/History

Hinduism was replaced by Islam, only for Hinduism to regain control again—one spiritual power rising against another. As Islamic Moguls gained power in the north, they sought to control India's south. Islamic raiding parties went to Golkonda to capture it. The solid stone walls of its citadel held off the warriors for eight months but finally fell to the Mogul forces.

The citadel increased and expanded in the sixteenth century to create a new city, Hyderabad. Hyderabad became a regional center for Islam and the seat of the wealthy Nizam (ruler) of Hyderabad. The Nizams ruled the area beginning in the eighteenth century and were allowed to rule the state during the time of British colonial rule.

In 1947 independence was granted to India by the British, and the Nizams called for an independent Islamic territory. But 85 percent of the city's population was Hindu at the time, and the Indian government in Delhi did not want a separate Islamic state within India. Hyderabad State became part of the Indian Union.

Today Hyderabad has grown, connecting itself with the neighboring city of Secunderabad. Combined, this metropolitan area is India's sixth largest city. Hyderabad is home to one of the largest Christian populations in India.

PRAYER POINTS

1. Pray that the minds of believers would be renewed, so that unbiblical thinking that has persisted in the traditional Christian community would cease.

2. Pray that the believers would become involved in cross-cultural evangelism and for a harvest among the largely unreached Muslims.

3. Pray that the Christian agencies, institutions, and teachers here would have a great spiritual impact on the city.

4. Vacation Bible Schools are being used to reach children. Pray for many children and parents to come to Christ.

5. Many beggars are in the city. Pray for them to come to Christ and to find work.

6. Pray for the vibrant pastors' and leaders' fellowship to grow and affect the city.

Meaning: named after the goddess Kali

Country: India, West Bengal State*

Population: 15,577,000

Living Standards: Among the world's lowest urban living standards

Religious Breakdown:
75.0% Hindu
22.0% Muslim
2.0% Christian
1.0% Other

Status of the Church: Two hundred churches, only one-quarter are Bengali-speaking

Major Religious Sites: Kali Temple, Sitambara Jain Temple, Tarakeshwar Temple, Nakhoda Mosque, St. Paul's Cathedral

Kolkata
(kohl-**kah**-tah)

City Significance/History

A little over three hundred years ago, Kolkata (formerly Calcutta) was just one of thousands of small villages in India. The British settled here in the late seventeenth century, and the village quickly grew into a city. Invasions by Indians made it necessary for the British to build a fort for protection. Kolkata became the capital and export center. William Carey pioneered a missionary movement here in 1793. The fall of the British caused great hardship in the city. Just to the east, East Pakistan (now Bangladesh) was established. Hindus moved west, and Muslims moved east.

The slums of Kolkata were made famous by the humble Mother Teresa.

She and others, like the Buntains, have brought hope and life to the slums, but increased migration to the city keeps the slums growing.

The local Bengali people worship Kali. Seen as the Earth Mother-Creator, she also has an evil side. Kali, translated "black," is the goddess of warfare, pestilence, blood sacrifice, and death. Kolkata, the city of Kali, lives up to its name. Many people come here to find a better life, but most end up never finding it—Kali, with her necklace of human heads, claims another victim to death. Yet the masses of people still come. Kolkata is India's third largest city and a city deep in bondage to its goddess.

PRAYER POINTS

1. The slums are some of the worst in the world. Pray that the poor can live in dignity and find the food they need. For most, the struggle for daily survival allows them no time for spiritual things.

2. The destructive god Kali is worshiped and appeased. Pray that God's power would be evident to the people living in bondage to Kali.

3. Pray that the value of human life, especially of females, will be recognized.

4. Pray for the Christian relief agencies, especially the hospitals and orphanages, that are ministering to the needy. Pray for strength and resources for the staff.

5. Pray for a Christian witness in the city's slums and among the unreached Muslims.

6. Pray for students studying in Bible colleges in Kolkata.

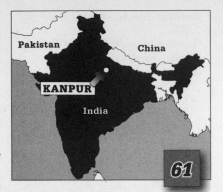

Meaning: "ear city"

Country: India, Uttar Pradesh Province

Population: 3,369,000

Living Standards: Five hundred thousand people in slums

Religious Breakdown:
77.8% Hindu
18.6% Muslim
0.8% Christian
2.8% Other

Status of the Church: Roman Catholic and Protestant fellowships, increased persecution

Major Religious Sites: JK Glass Temple, Memorial Church

Kanpur
(**kahn**-poor)

City Significance/History

From early on, northern India has been a Hindu territory. Millions of different gods and goddesses are worshiped and feared. The Mongol invaders brought Islam with them, and some of the people started to follow Islam. Kanpur was a city where a larger number of Indians turned to worship Allah.

Located on the Ganges River, Kanpur was a stronghold for the Indian mutiny in 1857 against the British. One uprising against the British saw the Indians massacre and dismember a British garrison. As British forces recaptured control of the city, they inflicted

The cow is one of their most sacred gods

much of the same treatment back on the Indians. They made them drink blood and eat beef (the cow is one of the most sacred gods for Hindus). They fed pork to the Muslims, which is considered extremely unclean by them. All this was done in retaliation for the uprising against the British rule.

Today the city has grown in size and has become one of the largest industrial cities in India. It has two universities and numerous technology institutes. Leather is an important industry in the city.

PRAYER POINTS

1. The few Christian workers here are laboring under very difficult circumstances. Pray for more evangelists and church planters to work in the harvest.

2. Pray that the Muslims, who are a large minority, may be reached with the gospel.

3. Most Christians are nominal and some are reverting to Hinduism. Pray that the knowledge of Jesus as Savior and Lord would grip their hearts.

4. Pray that the students in the city may hear the gospel and respond.

5. Pray that the residents of this spiritually dark province who migrate to Kanpur for work would encounter the gospel and come to faith in Jesus Christ.

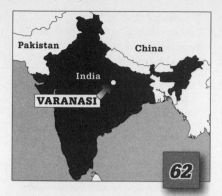

Meaning: "the city between two rivers"

Country: India, Uttar Pradesh Province

Population: 1,434,000

Living Standards: 10% live in slums

Religious Breakdown:
79.8% Hindu
19.6% Muslim
0.6% Christian

Status of the Church: twelve churches plus house fellowships

Major Religious Sites: Durga Temple, Golden Temple, Great Mosque of Aurangzeb, Sankatmochang Temple, Visvanatha Temple

Varanasi

(vuh-**rah**-nuh-**see**)

City Significance/History

Varanasi (also known as Banaras or Benares) has been a holy pilgrimage site for over two thousand years. Ten kilometers away at Saranath is where Buddha first preached on enlightenment. Hindus flock to the ghats (wide stairways), which provide access to wash, bathe, and even die in the Ganges River.

Relatives carry their dying loved ones to the river. Laying their frail body on one of the lower ghats (steps), they place the feet of the dying into the water. When the person dies, it is believed that he or she will go straight to heaven. This is important to many Hindus, who believe

Hindus flock to the Ganges

their dead relatives can come back as evil spirits to haunt them. Along one section of the ghats are the cremation pits. After the body has been cremated, the ashes are sprinkled on the holy Ganges River. Pilgrims bathe in the polluted Ganges, seeking to be healed.

Many Hindu priests live in Varanasi. As they walk around in deep trances, people seek them for blessings. Gurus have students who come from all over India to sit under their teaching, to meditate, and to learn Sanskrit.

The city is also home to a large minority of Muslims.

PRAYER POINTS

1. Pray that this holy city of Hinduism would become filled with the presence and power of the Holy Spirit.

2. Pray that the tiny minority of Christians, most of whom are nominal, would experience spiritual strengthening and renewal.

3. Pray that the millions of pilgrims visiting the Ganges River would find the living water given by Jesus.

4. Hindus here are among the world's most unreached people. Pray for workers to labor in this vast harvest field. Pray that the leaflets and Gospels that have been distributed would produce spiritual fruit.

5. Pray for more Muslim converts to Christianity. Pray for the growth of the few house fellowships that have developed.

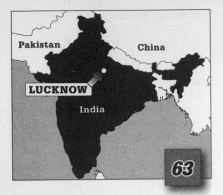

Meaning: "sign" or "mark"

Country: India, Uttar Pradesh State*

Population: 2,877,000

Living Standards: Uttar Pradesh State has largest number of poor in India; Lucknow living conditions are higher because of industry

Religious Breakdown:
76.8% Hindu
19.6% Muslim
0.8% Christian
2.8% Other

Status of the Church: Roman Catholic and Protestant churches

Major Religious Sites: Bara Imambara (Shiite grave site), Aurangzeb Mosque, Jami Masjid Mosque

Lucknow

(**luk**-now)

City Significance/History

The Muslim Moghuls established a growing power center in the area. They were replaced by still another Muslim group, the Oudh.

Along the Gomti River arose a small capital city for the Oudh Nawab rulers. These rulers came from a Persian background, not Mongol. From here, the Nawabs controlled north-central India for one hundred years. They developed the arts, fine culture, and traditional craftsmanship.

The British annexed the area in the mid-nineteenth century. The backlash from this annexation was an Indian uprising against the three thousand strong British diplomatic presence, including women and children. The Indians far outnumbered the British, who held out for three months in their compound, the Residency of the Nawab rulers. (The Residency was built for the glory of the Nawab rulers.) The Indian onslaught ended when more British troops broke through the Indian lines; however, two thousand of the British were dead.

Today the city still has a devoted Islamic population. Shiite holy men of the past are believed to have special power, even in their graves. Many Muslim people pray for strength and blessings at the tombs of these holy men.

PRAYER POINTS

1. Pray for growth in the small churches, that new believers can be taught and discipled.

2. There is an open door for evangelism at several strategic locations. Pray for a harvest to come from the bold witness at these sites.

3. Many East Asian Muslims come here to study. Pray for the establishment of a ministry to them.

4. Pray for reconciliation between the Muslims and Hindus and that the religious tensions would dissipate.

5. Pray for Christian workers seeking to reach various people groups in the city.

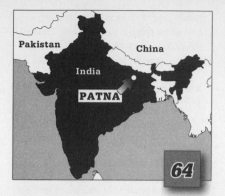

Meaning: "pale red son"

Country: India, Bihar State*

Population: 2,325,000

Living Standards: A few slum communities

Religious Breakdown:
71.0% Hindu
21.0% Muslim
4.0% Sikhs
0.5% Christian
3.5% Other

Status of the Church: Catholic, Protestant, and Orthodox

Major Religious Sites: Har Mandir (Sikh), Sher Shahi, Mahavir Mandir (Hindu), Husayt Shah Mosque

Patna

(**pat**-nuh)

City Significance/History

Founded in the sixth century BC, Patna is the third oldest city in India and a state capital. Over the centuries it has seen the rise and fall of major Indian empires, as well as a flow of various world religions.

Geographically, the city occupies a strategic site south of where the Ganges River meets two other rivers. This location provided natural protection. The city was originally founded as a fort, from which it could ward off attacks and raid enemy territories.

Patna has been the seedbed for religions. Besides fostering Hinduism, it berthed an offshoot—Jainism. The city has played a key role in the development of Buddhism; it is only one hundred kilometers from the place where Buddha reportedly reached enlightenment. Under the reign of Ashoka (third century BC), Patna became the center for the spread of Buddhism throughout Asia. Over one thousand years later, Muslims used it as a base to propagate Islam.

Today Hinduism is the predominant religion. Muslims make up about one-fifth of the population and the rest are Sikhs, Jains, and Buddhists. There are a few Roman Catholics and Protestant churches as well as a Syriac Orthodox Church.

PRAYER POINTS

1. In light of the city's religious history, pray that God would birth such a mighty movement of his Holy Spirit that Patna would again influence the entire subcontinent—this time for Jesus' glory.

2. Many Muslims who convert to Christianity revert back to Islam because of family and community pressure. Pray that the church would provide strong support and fellowship when Muslims turn to Christ.

3. Pray that the strife between Muslims and Hindus would cause disillusionment, leading them to the true Prince of Peace.

4. Pray that the hold of unemployment, poverty, and illiteracy would be broken and that people would be more responsive to the gospel.

5. Pray for unity among church congregations.

Meaning: "one temple by a tree"

Country: Nepal*

Population: 1,029,000

Living Standards: One-third live below the poverty line

Religious Breakdown:
69.0% Hindu
12.0% Traditional Ethnic
10.0% Buddhist
4.0% Christian
5.0% Other

Status of the Church: More than one hundred churches

Major Religious Sites: Pashupatinath Temple, Taleju Temple, Bodhanath Stupa, Swayambhunath Stupa, Kaba Aye Pagoda

Kathmandu

(kat-man-**doo**)

City Significance/History

Trade routes from Tibet and northern India passed through the high Himalayas and flowed past the foothills, where the fertile Kathmandu valley became an important trade center.

By the seventeenth century, the local Newari people refined much of the Hindu temple and worship art. The valley consisted of small city-states competing to outdo each other in art techniques and creativity. Many of the carved gods and temples took shape during this period.

One hundred years later, Nepal was unified by the first Gorka king. From this time, the metro area of Kathmandu grew as more and more villagers came from all over Nepal, the vast majority being Hindu.

The Bagmati River cuts through the valley on its way through the foothills of Nepal and meets the Ganges River many kilometers later. Along the river is Pashupatinath, the most holy Hindu temple in Nepal. Pilgrims from India come here because it is the holiest Shiva temple in the world. Shiva—the creator and destroyer, the shepherd and the bloodthirsty—is who the pilgrims seek. Protecting the entrance to Shiva's temple is Nandi, Shiva's golden bull.

Not many kilometers to the west is the Great Stupa of Bodhanath, the largest Buddhist temple in Nepal.

PRAYER POINTS

1. Pray for the removal of the barriers to Christianity in the minds of Hindu Nepalis.

2. Pray that the government would continue to guarantee freedom of religion and that the church will be able to evangelize without persecution.

3. The churches in the Kathmandu valley are clannish and divided. Pray that they would become unified in Christ.

4. Pray that believers would be delivered from superstitions and old ways of living, and that they would learn to walk in the Spirit.

5. Pray that the caste system, which separates people, would be brought down.

Meaning: unknown
Country: Bhutan*
Population: 87,000
Living Standards: Undeveloped subsistence economy, development potential
Religious Breakdown:
66.0% Buddhist
27.0% Hindu
4.0% Traditional Ethnic
2.0% Christian
1.0% Other
Status of the Church: A few small fellowships
Major Religious Sites: Tashichho Dzong, Chang Ganka Monastery, Cheri Monastery

Thimphu

(tim-**poo**)

City Significance/History

All throughout the Himalayas, flags and other pieces of cloth wave in the wind—Buddhist prayers continue to be offered by the moving cloths. The small Buddhist country of Bhutan, with its largest city and capital, Thimphu, has been left alone throughout history.

During the British occupation of India, British diplomats came through Thimphu seeking permission to move goods from Tibet through Bhutan into India. For periods of time there was no problem being part of this trade route. After the English left and China entered Tibet, Bhutan became a hidden country with Buddhist temples and monasteries dotting the mountains.

In Thimphu is the largest Buddhist center in the country, Tashichho Dzong. The name translates something close to "the fort of the glorious religion." (Similar dzongs are found throughout the country.) One half of the building is dedicated to Buddhism; the other half is used as a government center. From Tashichho, all the civil and religious administration is carried out for the whole country. From here the government is run out of the king's ornate throne room. A Buddhist monastery is also found at this dzong.

PRAYER POINTS

1. Tashichho Dzong is the power center of the country, administrating both religion and government. Pray that God would be known by the monks and political leaders.

2. Pray that the king would be favorable to Christianity and grant freedom to witness and worship. Pray that tentmakers could work without restrictions.

3. Pray for the protection of Bible translators and that translations into Dzongkha, Kebumtamp, and Sharchagpakha would be completed.

4. The Drukpa majority is strongly Buddhist with only a few hundred known believers. Pray for a dynamic indigenous church to be raised up.

5. Little Christian literature and no radio programming are available in the official Dzongkha language. Pray for the development of these essential tools.

India

Sri Lanka

COLOMBO ★

67

Meaning: "harbor"

Country: Sri Lanka*

Population: 678,000 (Colombo Metropolitan Region: 5,648,000)

Living Standards: Widespread poverty

Religious Breakdown:
64.0% Buddhist
15.0% Christian
13.0% Hindu
8.0% Muslim

Status of the Church: Mainly Roman Catholic; stagnant growth

Major Religious Sites: Kelaniya Raja Maha Vihara Temple, Vajiraramaya Temple, Grand Mosque

Colombo
(koh-**lum**-boh)

City Significance/History

Christian tradition holds that the apostle Thomas visited this area. Maritime Arabs in the eighth century established a port in Colombo for the export of cinnamon. Eight centuries later, the Portuguese replaced the Arabs and traded everything from cinnamon to elephants. The wide variety of spices attracted most traders.

The Portuguese, who brought Roman Catholicism, carved their seal of arms on a rock above the sea and built a fortress. The Dutch and British controlled the area until the British granted Sri Lanka independence in 1948. The growth of the city occurred during the British occupation, as the city continued to develop as a hub for Indian Ocean trade.

Colombo has become a refuge for the poor of Sri Lanka. Almost two-thirds of the huge metro population live in shanties where living conditions are extremely low. As the city grows, the poor are forced to live next to the canals and roadways. Some are displaced into the marshes and lowlands, where health conditions are poor.

One of the problems facing the government is child labor. Many poor families sell their children to the rich. These children work as domestic help, with the hope that they will receive food and clothing.

PRAYER POINTS

1. Pray for an increase in the standard of living so parents can support their children. Pray that the children who must work for the rich will not be exploited.

2. Pray for protection and strength for believers who are caught in the tension and violence between the Buddhist Sinhala and Hindu Tamil.

3. Pray for a renewed sense of calling in the national church and that evangelism and discipleship would replace compromise and nominal faith.

4. Conversions among the Buddhists and Hindus have produced a backlash. Pray that opposition and persecution would not hinder the ongoing witness to them.

5. Pray for unity and cooperation among churches and for the growth of evangelical fellowships.

EASTERN ASIA

EASTERN ASIA
MAJOR UNREACHED PEOPLES

City	Peoples
Taipei	Taiwanese, Hakka, Ami, Paiwan
Shenyang	Manchu, Korean, Mongolian, Hui
Changchun	Manchu, Korean, Hui, Mongolian
Urumqi	Uygur, Kazakh, Hui, Kirghiz
Lhasa	Tibetan, Blang, Bui
Lanzhou	Hui, Tibetan, Dongxaing
Beijing	Han Chinese, Hui, Manchu
Hohhot	Mongolian, Hui, Manchu
Tianjin	Han Chinese, Hui, Manchu, Bai
Taiyuan	Han Chinese, Hui, Manchu
Jinan	Han Chinese, Korean, Manchu, Mongolian
Nanjing	Zhaung, Yao, Dong, Miao
Xi'an	Han Chinese, Hui, Manchu
Chengdu	Han Chinese, Yi, Tibetan, Miao
Chongqing	Han Chinese, Yi, Tibetan, Tujia
Shanghai	Han Chinese, Hui, Bai
Wuhan	Han Chinese, Tujia, Buyi, Hui
Guangzhou	Han Chinese, Li, Zhaung, Yao
Hanoi	Vietnamese, Central Khmer, Muong, Hmong
Vientiane	Laotian, Tai, Khmer, Hmong
Phnom Penh	Khmer, Vietnamese, Cham, Mnong
Bangkok	Northern Thai, Southern Thai, Northern Khmer, Pattani Malay
Yangon	Burmese, Burmese Shan, Mon, Yangbye
Dhaka	Bengali, Sylhetti Bengali, Bihari
Kuala Lumpur	Malay, Chinese, Sarawak, Tamil
Jakarta	Buginese, Sasak, Achehnese, Rejang
Bandar Seri Begawan	Malay, Han Chinese, Than
Ulaanbaatar	Mongolian, Kazakh, Uighur
Pyongyang	Korean, Chinese
Sapporo	Japanese, Eta, Ryukyuan, Ainu
Tokyo-Yokohama	Japanese, Eta, Ryukyuan, Okinawan
Osaka-Kobe-Kyoto	Japanese, Eta, Ryukyuan, Ainu
Fukuoka-Kitakyushu	Japanese, Eta, Ryukyuan, Ainu

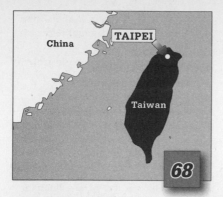

Meaning: "north Taiwan"

Country: Taiwan* (country status undesignated)

Population: 8,325,000

Living Standards: Economic stability

Religious Breakdown:
43.0% Chinese folk-religionist
26.5% Buddhist
12.6% Daoist
7.2% Christian
10.7% Other

Status of the Church: Mostly Protestant; stagnation in church growth

Major Religious Sites: Lungshan Temple, Hsing Tien Temple, Temple of Confucius

Taipei
(tai-pay)

City Significance/History

The Chinese, as early as the seventeenth century, sailed to Taiwan and settled in Taipei. As the Japanese expanded their influence southward, they made Taipei one of their administrative and economic centers. By World War II it had grown but remained mainly an agricultural hub where three rivers join.

After Japan was forced to surrender, the Chinese Communist movement continued to grow on mainland China. So the Nationalist Chinese, led by Chiang Kai-shek, were forced to retreat from the mainland to Taiwan. Taipei was chosen as the capital, and the city expanded. Universities and industries grew quickly as post-war peace gave rise to new hopes and dreams. Many wealthy Chinese fled in fear of the Communists taking all their wealth. These people invested in the development of the new city and nation.

Wise investments and development of industry and educational centers increased the wealth still farther. These advances attracted the rural population. In response, the government started building educational and industrial centers in other cities. This has discouraged villagers from relocating. But most still view Taipei as the city of gold, where riches can be found.

PRAYER POINTS

1. Pray that a spirit of sophistication that rejects Christianity can be broken among the young people so that witness among students will be fruitful.

2. There is a resurgence of Buddhism and animism. Pray that those who are seeking spiritual reality will find Jesus.

3. The official status of Taiwan has not been determined. Pray for peace as political issues between mainland China and Taiwan are worked out.

4. Pray for revival in the church and that national pastors and leaders will be raised up.

5. Pray for national and foreign missionaries to have renewed vision for reaching the people. Pray for the success of Christian ministries in Taiwan.

Meaning: "north bank of Shen River"

Country: China, Liaoning Province*

Population: 4,952,000

Living Standards: Economic growth in 2000s

Religious Breakdown:
42.0% Nonreligious
34.0% Chinese folk-religionist
16.0% Buddhist
2.0% Christian
6.0% Other

Status of the Church: House churches (majority), Roman Catholic, and TSPM (see Jinan on page 115 for TSPM explanation); many Korean Christians

Major Religious Sites: North Tomb (Beiling), East Tomb (Dongling), Gugong Imperial Palace

Shenyang
(shen-yahng)

City Significance/History

Shenyang is the historic cradle of the Manchu people. It was an important city for trade back in the eleventh century.

One reason the Great Wall of China was constructed was to protect the Ming Dynasty from foreign invasion. During the seventeenth century, the Manchus became a formidable and well-organized force, coming from China's northeast. The Ming reign was weakening, and the Manchus were able to conquer the whole country with very little opposition. Many of the leaders that were part of the Ming leadership were killed or submitted to the Manchus. The city became the Manchu capital in 1625.

Manchu men shaved their foreheads, and a long pigtail flowed down their backs. The Manchu Dynasty (also called the Qing Dynasty) lasted almost two centuries, expanding China's borders to greater lengths than before.

In the twentieth century the Russian and Japanese both occupied the area and started to develop the city as an industrial giant. The city's population exploded because of the converging of six railroads and the industrial expansion.

The Manchus conquered the whole country

PRAYER POINTS

1. The Manchu people have largely assimilated into Chinese culture, but some retain their old culture. Pray that they will encounter and respond to the gospel.

2. Pray for unity among the city's believers and that God will expose false believers within the church.

3. Political motives and connections motivate the older leaders in the Three-Self Patriotic Movement (TSPM). Pray that the younger leaders who seek to preach the gospel will prevail in the current power struggle.

4. Pray that the police will no longer harass and detain these young Christian leaders.

5. Pray that those migrating to the city for work will encounter the gospel.

Meaning: "eternal spring"

Country: China, Jilin Province*

Population: 3,400,000

Living Standards: Strong economy, rising population

Religious Breakdown:
40.0% Nonreligious
32.0% Chinese folk-religionist
14.0% Buddhist
8.0% Christian
6.0% Other

Status of the Church: House churches (majority), Roman Catholic, and TSPM; many Korean Christians

Major Religious Sites: Weihuaninggong Imperial Residence

Changchun
(chong-choon)

City Significance/History

Watchtowers top the many buildings of the tree-lined avenues of Changchun. Most of these buildings were built by the Japanese during their military occupation of this region from 1933 to 1945. The city was used for administrative headquarters and the capital of the Manchukou, a puppet government set up by Japan. Most of the electric lines were run underground to better protect them during this extremely traumatic time. The Japanese slaughtered many Chinese during their occupation.

The arrival of the Cultural Revolution brought persecution of Christians, and churches were closed. Although restrictions for churches to minister have been somewhat lifted, relatively few believers want to identify with the "official" church because of fear of persecution. The majority of Christians continue to meet in house churches.

Today Changchun is known for its university and automobile industry. It is also the site of one of China's most famous film studios.

Because of its proximity to North Korea, the population of Koreans living in the city is significant. When militant communism started to grip Korea, many Koreans fled across the border into the Jilin Province.

PRAYER POINTS

1. Pray for the growing church among the ethnic Koreans in and around the city — that they would zealously share their faith with unreached Koreans in the area.

2. Pray for the ethnic Korean Christians as they seek to contact family and friends back in North Korea. May they bring a bold witness to them.

3. Pray that the film industry would produce pro-Christian films.

4. Pray that Christian radio programming that is broadcast into the city would bring in a great harvest.

5. Pray that Bible study and teaching materials would become available to explain the gospel to students and professors at the university.

Meaning: "pleasant meadows"

Country: China, Xinjiang Uyghur Autonomous Region*

Population: 2,340,000

Living Standards: Strong economy and rising living standards

Religious Breakdown:
50.0% Nonreligious
25.0% Muslim
20.0% Chinese folk-religionist
0.4% Christian
4.6% Other

Status of the Church: House churches (majority), Roman Catholic, and TSPM; few Uygur believers

Major Religious Sites: Hongshan Pagoda, Tianchi (nearby sacred lake), Bogda Feng (nearby sacred mountain), Mingde Church

Urumqi
(oo-room-chee)

City Significance/History

In the far northwestern region of China, the people still have Mongol features, but Islam has traditionally been their religion. The Uyghurs, one of the area's ethnic peoples, have a mixture of Chinese and Turkish features. Throughout most of history, Urumqi was a small, dusty Uyghur village with little significance, part of the Silk Road.

At the end of World War II, the Communists started to change the look of the village. Concrete-block apartment buildings were built to provide housing, and smokestacks marked another factory on the wastelands at the edge of the desert. The Communists sent more than five million Han Chinese into Xinjiang Province, China's largest political unit, to dilute the Uygur's nationalistic feelings. During the Cultural Revolution of the late 1960s, they destroyed thousands of mosques. Many have since been rebuilt, but few Uyghur young people attend the mosque.

The region has become a nuclear test site, so the presence of the military has increased. Because of this, more Han have relocated here, and they now dominate government, industry, and business, a fact resented by the Uyghurs. A racial riot between the the Uyghur and the Han broke out in 2009.

PRAYER POINTS

1. Pray for openness to the gospel among the thirteen ethnic minorities, particularly the Muslim Uyghurs, Kyrgyz, and Kazakhs. Pray for reconciliation between these minorities and the Han Chinese, who make up 75 percent of the population.

2. Pray that the Han believers will reach out to their Muslim neighbors and demonstrate the love of Christ.

3. Muslim converts are subjected to great persecution and rejection. Pray that Uyghur fellowships would be established for strength and support.

4. Pray for spiritual strength, encouragement, and open doors to witness for foreign believers who have made their home in this remote city.

5. Pray for the completion and distribution of the New Testament and the distribution of the *Jesus* film in Uyghur.

Russia

Mongolia

LHASA   China

India

72

Meaning: "city of god"

Country: China, Tibet Autonomous Region*

Population: 122,000

Living Standards: Agriculture and tourism support economy; basic needs are met

Religious Breakdown:
90.0% Buddhist
8.1% Traditional Ethnic
1.3% Muslim
0.6% Christian

Status of the Church: Several house fellowships among the Han; a small number of Tibetan converts

Major Religious Sites: Potala Palace; Jokhang Temple; Sera, Drepung, and Nechung Monasteries

Lhasa

(**lah**-suh)

City Significance/History

The ancient religion of Tibet was Bon, a form of Shamanism. A shaman became a medium between the visible and invisible world. According to Bon, the world had three spheres: heaven, occupied by the Lha (gods); earth, mastered by Nagas (humans); and the underworld, inhabited by Tsen (demons).

The Potala Palace, built in the seventeenth century, remains one of the earth's most amazing structures. It embodies the heart of Tibetan Buddhism, both as a religion and a political force. Thousands of rooms house shrines, statues, and tombs of former Dalai Lamas. (The Dalai Lama is the traditional government ruler and the highest priest or god. After the Communist takeover, however, the Dalai Lama moved to India in 1959 and has since led the government in exile.) The palace is full of idols with spiritual significance. Maitreya is an enlightened Buddha yet to come, the wrath of Tara can be sought, and Amitayus will bring infinite life. These are only a few of the idols that find refuge, worship, and honor in the palace.

Rising early in the morning, monks and pilgrims climb the many stairs of the palace—repeatedly kneeling, rising, and taking a step—while chanting the same prayer over and over.

PRAYER POINTS

1. Pray for peace and resolution in this land which has been marked by unrest and violence between the Tibetans and Chinese.

2. Pray that Christians in exile will return and preach the gospel and encourage the believers. Pray also that the Dalai Lama, who is an influential spiritual leader around the world, would come to know Jesus.

3. Pray for open doors and wise distribution of the Scriptures in Tibetan.

4. Pray that monks initiated into the Tantra of Yamantaka at the Jokhang Temple would come into contact with the living Word and receive salvation.

5. Pray that the small house fellowships in the city would be strengthened and multiply throughout the Lhasa valley.

Meaning: "the fragrant city"
Country: China, Gansu Province*
Population: 2,785,000
Living Standards: Industry has increased living standards
Religious Breakdown:
   40.0% Nonreligious
   32.0% Chinese folk-religionist
   14.0% Buddhist
   10.0% Christian
   4.0% Other
Status of the Church: Several churches plus house fellowships
Major Religious Sites: White Pagoda, Temple of the Town Gods, Binglingsi Buddhist Caves

Lanzhou
(lahn-joh)

City Significance/History

Dust rises and blows over the city from the desert that runs from Lanzhou into Inner Mongolia. This haze, mixed with industrial pollution, covers the city—the capital of one of China's poorest provinces.

For historical traders crossing the desert, oasis villages provided stepping stones on their way from places as far away as Rome to find the valuable silk of the East. Lanzhou has been a crossroads city from the beginning. The trade routes went in all directions, bringing unusual travelers through the city. Silk went west with travelers; Buddhism was brought up from the south.

Lining the Yellow River, Lanzhou developed as a railroad link for goods going to other places, but it has now been transformed into an industrial center for northwest China.

The Yellow River provides water to desertlike but extremely fertile land. Crops of melons and other fruits have kept much of the population working, and since the 1960s China's atomic energy industry has been based in Lanzhou.

China's atomic energy industry headquarters

PRAYER POINTS

1. Pray for the gospel to come in power to this desert region of China, which is spiritually barren as well.

2. Pray for Christian teachers and workers to come to this city and region, which has low literacy levels and a high poverty rate.

3. Pray for a witness to the Hui people, who are ethnically Chinese but culturally Muslim. Pray that their traditional resistance to the gospel will be broken down.

4. Pray for the Holy Spirit to move among the Chinese soldiers who make up a large percentage of the population.

5. Pray that the leaders in this provincial capital would not persecute believers or hinder the growth of the church.

Russia

Mongolia

BEIJING

China

India

74

Meaning: "northern capital"
Country: China*
Population: 11,741,000
Living Standards: One of the China's most prosperous cities, but many poor migrants
Religious Breakdown:
43.0% Nonreligious
34.0% Chinese folk-religionist
16.0% Buddhist
1.4% Christian
5.6% Other
Status of the Church: Eight registered TSPM churches, thousands of house churches
Major Religious Sites: Fayuan Si Temple, Niu he Muslim Temple, Guangji Temple, Mao Zedong Memorial Hall, Temple of Heaven

Beijing
(bay-jing)

City Significance/History

Beijing's location on the edge of China's Northern Plain made it a strategic military location for the control of China's north. Brutal invasions have struck Beijing throughout history.

Genghis Khan, coming down from Mongolia, slaughtered and destroyed the city in the thirteenth century. From the rubble arose Khanbaliq, "Khan's Town." His grandson, Kublai Khan, ruled all of China, his capital being Khanbaliq. Corruption and fraud destroyed the Khan's reign, and the Ming Dynasty grew in its place.

The Forbidden City, the Temple of Heaven, and the Ming Tombs are lasting examples of the grandeur and exclusionist attitude of the Ming power base. Reigning from the fourteenth to seventeenth century, the Ming Dynasty fell apart, allowing the Qing Dynasty to take over China and set up their capital in Beijing, only later to become a victim of the Cultural Revolution in 1911.

After the Japanese were defeated in World War II, Mao Zedong took power and started the People's Republic of China, turning all of China over to Communism. With Communism came roads, railways, one language, and universal education. Beijing developed greatly as China's capital and cultural and educational center. It is China's second largest city.

PRAYER POINTS

1. From Beijing, 1.3 billion people are governed. Pray for God's purposes to be worked through the government, and for Christian officials to to be raised up.

2. Pray for the safety of persecuted house church leaders who seek to minister for Christ in this tightly controlled environment. Pray that believers will have discernment about how and to whom they should share the gospel.

3. Pray that disillusioned university intellectuals in their search for truth would discover Christ. Also pray for the effective follow-up and nurture of returned intellectuals who have become Christians while studying abroad.

4. Pray that the poor will not be overlooked in this prosperous city. Pray for Christian ministries that are seeking to meet the physical and spiritual needs of these people.

Meaning: "green city"
Country: China, Inner Mongolia Autonomous Region*
Population: 1,878,000
Living Standards: Economic center of impoverished region
Religious Breakdown:
　38.0% Nonreligious
　29.0% Chinese folk-religionist
　13.0% Christian
　10.0% Buddhist
　10.0% Muslim
Status of the Church: House churches, Roman Catholics, three TSPM churches; few Mongol Christians
Major Religious Sites: Wuta Si (Five Pagoda Temple), Da Zhao Temple, Xilitu Zhao Temple, Great Mosque

Hohhot
(hoh-hoht)

City Significance/History

Cold winter wind blew a fresh layer of snow against the north side of the yurt (nomadic tent home). To avoid the cold, horses were tied on the south side of the small circular home. Inside, the goat milk was still warm. Ogadai remembered the summertime, when the grasslands provided plenty of food. Tomorrow he would leave his family and trek the day's journey to Hohhot. He wanted to offer a goat to the sun god, and he heard that a Tibetan Buddhist monk was in town.

Gods are everywhere—in the rivers, stars, sun, and moon. Nature offers infinite gods to worship and revere.

Ogadai knew that Mongol priests in Hohhot could make an offering acceptable to the different gods. And the Buddhist monk could offer spiritual insight. In Hohhot Ogadai would also be able to trade skins for salt and other goods.

Such was the life of a nomadic Mongol herdsman a thousand years ago. Hohhot started as a trading post and a place of temples. As China and the former USSR fought over Mongolia, Inner Mongolia became part of China, with Hohhot being the administrative and educational center. Mongols are a minority people in their own homeland.

PRAYER POINTS

1. Pray for the gospel to be planted and bear fruit among the historically resistant Mongols. Pray for the production of a Mongolian-script New Testament.

2. Pray that radio ministry directed to the Mongols might have an increased harvest.

3. Pray that the nationalistic aspirations of the Mongols might be realized in the coming of the kingdom of God to their people.

4. Illiteracy has been an obstacle to the Han Chinese Christians growing in their faith. Pray for increased understanding of God's Word among these believers.

5. Pray for teachers to help raise the literacy level of the residents.

Meaning: "ford of heaven"

Country: China

Population: 7,468,000

Living Standards: Stable economy has provided basic needs

Religious Breakdown:
43.0% Nonreligious
34.0% Chinese folk-religionist
16.0% Buddhist
1.3% Christian
5.7% Other

Status of the Church: Majority Roman Catholic, some house fellowships

Major Religious Sites: Grand Mosque, Dabeiyuan Monastery, Confucius Temple, Tianhou Temple

Tianjin
(tyahn-jin)

City Significance/History

Dating back to the third century BC, when China's history was known as the Warring States period, Tianjin has had a militant reputation. Many saw this fortified city as strategic because it was ideal as a trade port and the main link with Beijing. France, Britain, Belgium, Germany, Russia, Japan, Italy, and the U.S.-ruled Tianjin because of their interest in Far East trade. For periods, some of these countries had a significant military and diplomatic presence in the city at the same time.

The foreign invaders all left their mark on the city. Different buildings have

Foreign invaders all left their mark

French, German, or Italian features. Japan, during World War II, helped the city move forward as an industrial giant.

The Hai River allowed for ships to travel to the city, but heavy silting moved the main port downstream. The Japanese started dredging and expanding the port, with the work finally being finished by the Communists. Now Tianjin handles a great number of goods, making it one of the busiest areas in China. It is the country's sixth largest city and one of its busiest shopping centers, with Commercial Street servicing almost 700,000 shoppers daily.

PRAYER POINTS

1. Pray that the Christians will grow in boldness and faith and that believers holding political positions would have wisdom and an effective witness.

2. Pray that evangelization resources and workers inside and outside the country will be called to Tianjin, and that the city might truly become a gateway to the kingdom of heaven in that region of China.

3. Pray that the response to Christian radio broadcasts and the *Jesus* film would greatly increase and that Christian literature would become more accessible.

4. Pray that disillusionment with Communism and ancient practices would be replaced with hope in Jesus Christ.

5. Pray that the Christians working among the oil rig workers in the Bohai Sea would have an opportunity to evangelize their coworkers.

Meaning: "great plain"

Country: China, Shanxi Province*

Population: 3,104,000

Living Standards: Pollution and some urban slums

Religious Breakdown:
40.0% Nonreligious
32.0% Chinese folk-religionist
14.0% Buddhist
8.5% Christian
5.5% Other

Status of the Church: Twelve Protestant churches, many Roman Catholics

Major Religious Sites: Chongshan Monastery, Yongzhou Monastery, Jinci Temple Complex, Twin Pagoda Temple

Taiyuan
(tai-ywahn)

City Significance/History

From its earliest foundations, the city has been a place of conflict. Twenty-seven of the temples at one time were dedicated to the god of war — violence was prevalent. As one military campaign after another swept through China, Taiyuan was always in the way. Almost every invading force conquered the city.

In the early 1900s, the emperor of China gave an edict that all foreigners should be killed, and the Boxer Rebellion was under way. To carry out the edict, soldiers from the Chinese secret society traveled from city to city killing foreigners. Special targets were the "evil ones" — missionaries.

Two hundred missionaries were martyred

When the troops arrived at Taiyuan, they found a walled city. The troops closed the gates, trapping everyone inside. The troops hunted down and beheaded the evil ones; around two hundred missionaries were martyred. But the 3,000-member Chinese local church lost even more, as many of them tried to protect the missionaries or wanted to identify with Christ and not the Rebellion.

Taiyuan is the industrial center of the region and home to nine institutes of higher learning.

PRAYER POINTS

1. Pray that from the blood of the martyrs a strong and faithful witness will grow and produce fruit of righteousness greater than the evil of the past.

2. Shanxi Province is one of the least evangelized provinces in China, and the church is often repressed. Pray for evangelists to be raised up and that Taiyuan would become a center for the dissemination of the gospel.

3. Pray for the safe delivery of Bibles and Christian books that come through Taiyuan on their way to believers in the surrounding countryside.

4. Pray for believers enduring extremely harsh conditions in the coal mines around the city, that their joyful witness would draw others to Christ.

5. Pray that worship of Guanyin, the goddess of mercy, would be replaced by worship of the true God of mercy.

114

Meaning: "south of the River Ji"

Country: China, Shandong Province*

Population: 2,914,000

Living Standards: Stable economy, one of China's wealthiest provinces

Religious Breakdown:
40.5% Nonreligious
32.5% Chinese folk-religionist
14.5% Buddhist
6.5% Christian
6.0% Other

Status of the Church: Mainly house churches, some TSPM and Roman Catholic churches

Major Religious Sites: Thousand Buddha Mountain, Shentong Monastery, Divine Rock Temple

Jinan
(jee-nahn)

City Significance/History

Jinan is often referred to as "the city of springs," a reference to its 102 natural springs. Their source is the Lake of Great Purity outside the city. Huge dikes protect the city from the Yellow River's periodic flooding. The Shanghai-to-Beijing railway runs through Jinan, providing income and trade.

In China there are two main divisions in the church: the registered church and the unregistered church. The Three-Self Patriotic Movement (TSPM) is the government-controlled organization of Protestant churches. The unregistered Protestant population, which makes up the majority of Christians in China, consists of underground house churches.

Through the TSPM and a similar organization for Catholics, the Chinese government seeks to control the church in the country. The government has placed pastors in the TSPM churches and has put restrictions on the teaching and activities of the church. Despite some leaders' concessions to the government, there are many faithful Christians who serve in TSPM churches. Both registered churches and unregistered house churches continue to grow throughout China.

A TSPM seminary is located in Jinan, and Chinese Christians come here to be trained. A large number of house churches are also in the city.

PRAYER POINTS

1. The government has begun to allow Bibles to be printed in China, most of which go to the spiritually hungry believers in the TSPM churches. Pray that these Bibles will produce a great harvest and true worshipers.

2. Pray for the TSPM seminary. May God use this building and these students to increase his name and glory in all of China. Pray for biblical teaching and training.

3. Pray that residents of this city of springs may come to know the Source of living water, who brings true righteousness and purity.

4. Pray for spiritual revival in this educational and industrial center.

5. Tai Shan, one of China's five sacred mountains, rises one hundred kilometers south of the city. Pray that the spiritual power behind this stronghold would be broken.

Meaning: "southern capital"
Country: China, Jiangsu Province*
Population: 3,813,000
Living Standards: Economic growth
Religious Breakdown:
39.0% Nonreligious
31% Chinese folk-religionist
13% Buddhist
11.0% Christian
6.0% Other
Status of the Church: A center of Christianity in China, much church growth
Major Religious Sites: Linggu Temple, Qinhuai Confucian Temple, Ming Tomb and Sun Yat Sen Mausoleum, Fuzimiao Confucian Center, Revolutionary Martyrs Monument

Nanjing
(nahn-jing)

City Significance/History

As its name suggests, Nanjing has been the capital of China in the past. For economic and military reasons, the city has been selected and rejected as the capital.

In the nineteenth century the Taiping Revolution, a Chinese Christian army, succeeded in controlling most of southern China — only to have the Qing Dynasty, with the help of foreign powers, halt the revolution.

The church continued to grow, but with the Cultural Revolution the church went largely underground. Fear of death or imprisonment, and suspicion of the

Small house churches worshiped quietly and in fear

TSPM's connection to the government, sent many believers into hiding. Small house churches met in many different locations, worshiping quietly and in fear. For fifty years the house church movement has continued to grow. The number of TSPM believers in Jiangsu Province is now over one million; the large number of house church believers is not known. Hunger for the Word of God is strong. Nanjing is the location of a well-known TSPM seminary as well as Amity Press, which has printed millions of Bibles distributed around China.

PRAYER POINTS

1. Pray for the students and faculty at Jingling Union Theological Seminary, that they would desire to serve God and would be open to his leading.

2. Ask God to bless the correspondence and extension courses offered by the seminary for believers in towns and villages around China.

3. Pray for increased production of Bibles by the Amity Foundation, that they would get into the hands of believers hungering for God's Word.

4. Pray that house church believers will have the freedom to worship outside the TSPM and that they might receive Bibles from the official church without having to register.

5. Pray for continued growth and revival of believers in both the TSPM and house churches.

Russia
Mongolia
XI'AN
China
India
80

Meaning: "western peace"
Country: China, Shaanxi Province*
Population: 4,178,000
Living Standards: Growing economy
Religious Breakdown:
　41.0% Nonreligious
　33.0% Chinese folk-religionist
　15.0% Buddhist
　5.0% Christian
　6.0% Other
Status of the Church: Significant growth in recent decades, location of ancient Nestorian church
Major Religious Sites: Temple of Great Maternal Grace, Jianfu Temple, Ba Man An, Big Wild Goose Pagoda, Great Mosque

Xi'an
(shee-ahn)

City Significance/History

Today cities like Beijing and Shanghai are well known to most people. Three thousand years ago Xi'an was the Rome of the East. Traders came along the Silk Road from Rome, Persia, or Central Asia to do business in this great city. Merchants, artists, and soldiers walked the streets. Priests and emperors were honored and worshiped. The city was the capital for thirteen ancient dynasties—as one would fall, another would rise. The Silk Road also facilitated the eastward expansion of Buddhism into China.

In the eighth century, two million people might have lived in the metro area of Xi'an. But weakness in the Tang Dynasty permitted Turkish and Tibetan invaders to break up the taxation and wealth base of the dynasty. China was split into independent political states once again. The city declined quickly and never rose to be the national capital again.

The Communist government, in its effort to decentralize industry from the eastern megacities, has developed Xi'an into an industrial center. This has resulted in tremendous population growth in the past fifty years. The government has constructed many buildings, turned temples into factories or stores, and greatly improved the railways and roads.

PRAYER POINTS

1. The Nestorian Tablet, the record of Christianity's introduction to China in the seventh century, is housed at the provincial museum. Pray that this stone would speak prophetically to the people regarding their Christian heritage.

2. Pray that in this city of peace the true Prince of Peace might be known.

3. Pray for God's blessing on the unofficial house churches in and around Xi'an as they train hundreds of evangelists and leaders.

4. Pray that the pioneer church planting efforts of these evangelists throughout central China would be successful.

5. Pray that the city's Muslim quarter might be reached with the gospel.

6. Pray that TSPM members would know Christ as Savior and the Bible as God's Word.

Meaning: "perfect city"

Country: China, Sichuan Province*

Population: 4,266,000

Living Standards: Strong economy because of agricultural and technology industries

Religious Breakdown:
41.0% Nonreligious
33.0% Chinese folk-religionist
14.0% Buddhist
6.0% Christian
6.0% Other

Status of the Church: Two large TSPM churches, numerous house churches

Major Religious Sites: Baoguan Monastery, Wenshu Monastery, Marquis Wu Temple, Qingyang Gong Temple (Taoist)

Chengdu
(chung-doo)

City Significance/History

Jade and pearls are not the real riches of China—rice, wheat, soybeans, and silk bring the most wealth. Chengdu is the capital of the most populous province, Sichuan, which produces more rice and other grains than any other province. The fertile soil allows for agriculture to play a major role in the people's livelihood, and silk brings in further wealth.

Du Fu, a bright student, studies to take his college entrance exam. If he makes it into university, he will have a secure future. One of his friends failed the test, not so much because of lack of knowledge, but because of the extreme pressure that rides on this one test.

Du Fu leaves his parent's apartment on the third floor and walks down the poorly lit stairs. Mounting his bike, he heads for Wenshu Monastery. Wenshu is the god of wisdom, and it would be foolish not to offer incense before him. Fighting with other bikes for the right of way, Du Fu makes the left turn leading to Wenshu. He passes the fortune-teller, stopping only briefly to buy incense, then parks his bike.

Finally, before the statue of Buddha that came from Tibet at some earlier date, he lights three sticks of incense and bows gracefully at the waist. The exam grips his mind as he petitions for wisdom.

PRAYER POINTS

1. Many mission agencies are represented here, and each agency has its own view on sharing the gospel. Pray for unity and cooperation between Christians.

2. Pray for the safety of house church believers who face substantial repression from the Religious Affairs Bureau, the TSPM, and police.

3. Pray for an effective witness to Chengdu's floating population of migrant laborers from the surrounding villages.

4. Pray for openness among the students interested in books about Christianity.

5. The Marquis Wit Temple holds the history of three gods, with one still influencing most Chinese today. Pray that this influence binding the people would be broken.

6. Missionaries and tentmakers here battle loneliness, depression, and frustration. Pray for a release from all demonic oppression.

Meaning: "repeated good luck"

Country: China, Sichuan Province

Population: 6,690,000

Living Standards: Stable living standards in urban center, rapid population growth

Religious Breakdown:
41.0% Nonreligious
33.0% Chinese folk-religionist
14.0% Buddhist
6.0% Christian
6.0% Other

Status of the Church: 56 TSPM churches, some Roman Catholic and house churches

Major Religious Sites: Luo Han Temple, Beiwenquan Temple Complex

Chongqing
(chung-ching)

City Significance/History

Chongqing was established on the peninsula created by the confluence of the Jialing and the Yangtze Rivers. Around 200 BC, the Ba Kingdom used the peninsula as a capital and important trade center. The peninsula provided natural protection on three sides to resist outside invasion.

The Yangtze River is one of the main waterways across China and the world's third-longest river. The river connects Chongqing to Shanghai. Barges dock at Chaotiamen, where dock workers balance bamboo poles on their shoulders to unload the cargo. On the banks of the river, smokestacks spew pollution into the air. Behind the smoke, the hills of the city rise and homes can be seen.

Even though the Japanese heavily bombed the city during World War II, it still retains some of its ancient homes, narrow alleys, and winding stairways. Many refugees from the northeast fled before the murderous Japanese forces as they moved south. The population of Chongqing grew to almost two million.

After the war, peace treaties were signed, and the city became the most industrialized city in southwestern China. Industrial growth, a north–south trade location, and a river hub have enabled the city to swell to nearly seven million people.

PRAYER POINTS

1. Pray for believers seeking to establish the church in this transportation center, that it would become a hub for spreading the gospel in southwestern China.

2. Chongqing has traditionally been a bastion of Buddhism. Pray that this stronghold would be broken so that the light of the gospel might shine forth.

3. Pray that TSPM members might grow in their walk with the Lord and in their knowledge of the Bible.

4. Pray for workers to reach out to the Tibetans living in Sichuan Province and that Tibetan churches would be established.

5. Pray that worshipers at Luo Han Temple, who seek to be released from greed and hate, would realize only Christ can forgive sin and give release from condemnation.

Meaning: "upper ocean"

Country: China

Population: 15,789,000

Living Standards: Incomes and living standards have increased

Religious Breakdown:
35.0% Nonreligious
29.0% Chinese folk-religionist
17.5% Christian
13.0% Buddhist
5.5% Other

Status of the Church: 80 TSPM churches, strong Roman Catholic population, thousands of house church

Major Religious Sites: Longhua Temple, Temple of Town Gods, Jade Buddha Temple, First Communist Party Congress Site

Shanghai
(shang-hai)

City Significance/History

Shanghai's strategic location marked this unimportant, small weaving and fishing village as one destined to be China's largest city. The flowing Yangtze River meets the Pacific Ocean just south of Shanghai, connecting the city with far western Tibet and other cities in between. Trading has made it the third largest port in the world.

The British, followed by the French and Japanese, opened the city for their own interests in the 1800s. These foreign entities built autonomous power centers next to each other, in and around Shanghai. With foreign wealth and cheap local labor, the village grew to one million by 1900. The city became highly Westernized as foreigners built buildings in their own styles. Chinese servants, child slave labor, and prostitution became part of the imprint of Westernization.

After World War II, the Communists chose Shanghai to become the first Cultural Revolution "model city." Rehabilitation of opium addicts and the outlawing of child slave labor credit their efforts.

As China's largest city, Shanghai faces overcrowding and poverty in the streets, although the government has actively sought to improve living standards. In 1999 one thousand house churches were forcibly shut down, but Shanghai remains a Christian center in China.

PRAYER POINTS

1. Pray for the university students who seek meaning in life. Pray that their openness to hearing the gospel will lead them to become followers of Christ.

2. Prosperity and materialism have gripped the hearts of the people, with money becoming the most important factor in their lives. Pray against this spirit of greed.

3. Sexual lust and prostitution characterized pre-Revolution Shanghai. These influences are again seeking to undermine the moral fabric of Chinese society. Pray that this spirit of decadence is broken over the city once and for all.

4. Pray that the TSPM churches would seek to uphold biblical doctrines, not political ideas or agendas.

5. Pray for the continued growth of house churches despite government opposition.

Meaning: names of three cities combined

Country: China, Hubei Province*

Population: 7,542,000

Living Standards: Stable economy, many people with low incomes

Religious Breakdown:
41.0% Nonreligious
33.0% Chinese folk-religionist
14.0% Buddhist
6.0% Christian
6.0% Other

Status of the Church: Government repression, a few TSPM churches, strong house churches

Major Religious Sites: Guiyuan Temple, Hongshan Pagoda

Wuhan
(woo-hahn)

City Significance/History

Wuhan's name is a combination of the names of three cities—Wuchang (Wu) and Hanyang and Hankou (han)—that were finally unified in 1957. Wuchang, on the east bank of the Yangtze River, grew during the Han Dynasty as a regional capital and fortified city.

On the west side of the Yangtze, Hankou was only a village until the city opened for foreign trade. Russians, British, French, Germans, and Japanese set out to establish regional headquarters here. The foreign money turned Hankou into an industrial center in the interior of China. Foreign presence enabled mission agencies to send more workers into the interior. China Inland Mission pioneered the work in Wuhan using both overseas missionaries and national workers.

Next to Hankou but separated by the smaller Han River, Hanyang had slow beginnings. Hanyang's growth did not come until late in the nineteenth century, when industrial manufacturers built iron and steel plants. Japan's invasion totally destroyed most of the heavy industry. As rebuilding took place, many of the factories were tooled for light industry.

Today Wuhan is the most important industrial and commercial center in central China.

PRAYER POINTS

1. Pray that TSPM churches, such as Rong Guang Tang (Glory Church), would be filled with the glory and power of the Lord.

2. Pray for anointed Christian witness to the Chinese military, which has a strong presence in Hubei Province.

3. The province is less than 3 percent Christian. Pray for the evangelists laboring here, that the Holy Spirit would bring a great harvest.

4. Pray for the effectiveness of foreign Christian professionals teaching in the city. Pray that God would call more teachers willing to endure the hardships of living here in order to have a witness to students.

5. Pray against renewed interest in traditional folk religion and superstitious practices.

Meaning: "capital of a large region"

Country: China, Guangdong Province*

Population: 9,447,000

Living Standards: Expanding economy

Religious Breakdown:
41.0% Nonreligious
33.0% Chinese folk-religionist
15.0% Buddhist
5.0% Christian
6.0% Other

Status of the Church: Government repression, few TSPM churches

Major Religious Sites: Guangxiao Church, Hualin Temple, Wuxian Guan Temple, Six Banyan Trees Temple, Huaisheng Mosque

Guangzhou
(gwahng-joh)

City Significance/History

Legend tells that the city started after five goats with rice stalks in their mouths descended from heaven. The gods gave the rice and goats as a symbol of freedom from famine, but famines have still come. Guangzhou is also known as Yangcheng ("goat city") and as Canton.

More than any other city in China, Guangzhou has been the gateway for trade into China. As early as the second century, traders from the Roman Empire and India came to exchange goods. In the sixteenth century, Jesuit missionaries established a work in the city. The next few centuries brought more traders and foreign powers to the area. Robert Morrison, the first Protestant missionary, entered China through Guangzhou in 1807. By the time Mao closed the door to missions, a total of one million Christians were in the province.

Opium became an obsession for the wealthy Chinese. The British brought opium from India to meet the ever-growing demands of the Chinese addicts. The emperor of China finally ordered the city's regional head to get rid of the British. At the conclusion of the Opium War in 1842, the Chinese surrounded the British, killing many and driving the remaining out of the area. The city's troubling history with foreign influence has led to resistance to the gospel.

PRAYER POINTS

1. Pray for the growth and outreach of the harassed house churches and for the safety of their pastors.

2. Ask God to soften the hearts of the Religious Affairs Bureau officials who are antagonistic toward believers who remain outside the TSPM umbrella.

3. Pray that the gospel can be ministered effectively in the midst of social change, economic prosperity, and new ideas and trends flooding in from the outside.

4. Pray that students at the theological seminary affiliated with the TSPM Dong Shan Church would be called as pastors and evangelists.

5. Children are often used as tools for getting money. Pray for these children in bondage to begging. Pray also for the women caught in a life of prostitution.

Meaning: "the city at the river's bend"

Country: Vietnam*

Population: 4,723,000

Living Standards: Economic growth, highest living standards in country

Religious Breakdown:
49.0% Buddhist
19.0% Nonreligious
11.0% New Religionist
10.0% Traditional Ethnic
10.0% Christian

Status of the Church: Mainly Roman Catholic, much government persecution

Major Religious Sites: Chua Mot Cot (One Pillar Pagoda), Dien Huu Pagoda, Quan Su Pagoda, Ho Chi Minh Mausoleum

Hanoi
(ha-**noi**)

City Significance/History

For one thousand years, Hanoi has housed emperors and government officials. Under the Emperor Ly Thai To, the site was known as Souring Dragon. By the twentieth century, the French ruled Indo-China from their regional capital at Hanoi. The French colonial period inspired many Vietnamese to desire a free and independent homeland. The French suppressed a number of uprisings, but Marxist-Leninist revolutionary theory was taking root among the educated.

During World War II, power control of Indo-China changed from France to Japan, while the Communist Party grew in northern Vietnam. The following years saw the Vietnamese Communists take power, dividing the country between north and south in civil war. This war escalated into the Vietnam War, where cities and villages of civilians were destroyed to kill a few of the enemy's forces. In the end, the Communist north gained control of the whole country. Slowly the civil war gave rise to peace under Communism.

Four decades of suffering have started to allow greater freedom for a market economy. Religious figures (Buddhist and Catholic) have been imprisoned in recent years because they represented voices against Communist oppression.

PRAYER POINTS

1. Pray that more Bibles will be printed locally and distributed throughout the country.

2. Pressure by security forces on unregistered churches is growing. The government officially has loosened its rigid grip on religion, but police continue to raid churches. Pray for believers to have freedom to worship without harassment.

3. As business relations normalize with the outside world, pray for tentmakers to be called to work in the city.

4. Pray for a new generation of pastors to be raised up, and that the study materials and books needed to train them will become available.

5. Pray that the strongholds of Communism and Buddhism would yield to the power of the Holy Spirit.

Meaning: "city of sandalwood"

Country: Laos*

Population: 747,000

Living Standards: Subsistence economy

Religious Breakdown:
53.0% Buddhist
38.0% Traditional Ethnic
4.0% Nonreligious
4.0% Christian
1.0% Other

Status of the Church: Steadily growing, about half Protestant and half Roman Catholic

Major Religious Sites: Great Sacred Stupa, Wat Si Muang, Wat Ong Teu Mahawihan, Wat Sok Pa Luang, Wat Si Saket

Vientiane
(vyen-**tyahn**)

City Significance/History

The Mekong River and fertile plains made Vientiane a natural site for the Lao people to settle and start a small kingdom. Tradition tells that the city was established in the sixteenth century, when Wat Si Muang's pillar was laid.

A sacrifice was needed

Buddhist religious leaders wanted to build a new wat (sacred place where monks live) with a stone pillar as the centerpiece and Buddhas surrounding. A hole was dug, and a rope balanced the selected stone pillar above it; however, a sacrifice was needed. Gongs called the villagers to the site. Whether voluntary or not, a pregnant woman jumped into the hole and was crushed under the heavy pillar. The temple's name means "sacred city."

The lack of military power allowed the area to be overrun by every neighboring empire. The Thai, Chinese, Vietnamese, and later the French, Americans, and Russians all left their mark on the city. Since the sixteenth century, it has been a capital, but as early as the second century Buddhist monks passed this way.

The Communists have held power since 1975. Even though most of the country is very fertile, Laos has an extremely poor standard of living.

PRAYER POINTS

1. The church suffered much under Communism, with many believers falling away or backsliding. Pray for reconciliation and unity in the body of Christ.

2. Pray that all restrictions against public evangelism, church building, and missionaries will be lifted.

3. Pray for the tentmakers working in the city and that opportunities to present the gospel would arise.

4. Most of the church's trained leaders left in 1975. Pray for national pastors and teachers to be equipped and that training materials would become available.

5. Many indigenous people and villages in Laos have begun to turn to Christ. Pray that the indigenous Christians would spread the gospel into Vientiane and other cities.

Meaning: "the hill of a woman named Penh"

Country: Cambodia (Kampuchea)*

Population: 1,651,000

Living Standards: Low standard of living despite country's economic growth

Religious Breakdown:
85.0% Buddhist
4.7% Traditional Ethnic
3.0% Chinese folk-religionist
2.3% Christian
5.0% Other

Status of the Church: Increased freedom to worship, new churches

Major Religious Sites: Wat Phnom, Silver Pagoda, Wat Qunalom Monastery, Nur ul-Ihsan Mosque, Independence Monument

Phnom Penh

([puh]**nahm-pen**)

City Significance/History

In the mid-fifteenth century, the Khmer people were fighting the Thai, a long-standing enemy, as were the Vietnamese. The Thai captured the city of Angkor, causing the Khmer to relocate to Phnom Penh. Over one hundred years earlier, a woman named Penh had found a Buddha in one of the three rivers that run through the area. She placed the Buddha on the highest hill as a holy pagoda.

Battles with the Thai and Vietnamese continued, along with occupations by the Spanish and French. Catholic monks arrived with the Westerners.

Slowly the Communist Khmer Rouge started to take over rural areas. By the 1960s they controlled provincial capitals, and in 1975 Phnom Penh fell into their hands. The Communists wanted to rid the country of all religion. Buddhist monks were killed, and of the estimated 10,000 Christians in Phnom Penh, the vast majority were stabbed to death. The Khmer Rouge killed many people, including the educated, because they wanted to "purify" the Khmer people from outside influence.

In 1978 Vietnam sent troops into Phnom Penh and drove out the Khmer Rouge. More than ten years of occupation and conflict ensued. The United Nations worked to establish peace in the 1990s.

PRAYER POINTS

1. Pray for unity among the local church leaders as well as the Christian leaders from other countries who work in Phnom Penh.

2. Pray for protection of the body of Christ from materialism, corruption, wrong doctrine, and competition.

3. Pray that God will raise up more Christian leaders to disciple the harvest that is pouring into the kingdom of God. Youth workers are especially needed.

4. Pray that God will grant wisdom and finance to Christians who are willing to pioneer practical projects to rebuild the city and the lives of the people.

5. Many innocent people were tortured by the Khmer Rouge in prisons like Tuol Sleng. Pray for healing of the victims and forgiveness for former enemies.

Meaning: known as the "city of angels"

Country: Thailand*

Population: 6,918,000

Living Standards: Some slum communities

Religious Breakdown:
86.0% Buddhist
6.0% Muslim
3.0% Christian
2.0% Traditional Ethnic
3.0% Other

Status of the Church: Very slow growth in Catholic and Protestant churches

Major Religious Sites: Wat Arun, City Pillar Shrine, Reclining Buddha Temple, Golden Buddha Temple, Marble Temple, Emerald Buddha Temple, Wat Saket

Bangkok
(**bang**-kahk)

City Significance/History

Bangkok (or Krung Thep) began as a small village by the Chao Phya River in the eighteenth century and later became the capital of Thailand. Now over eight million people make their home in the vast sprawl of waterways and streets of Bangkok. The city's amazing growth is due primarily to the heavy influx of poor rural migrants.

Buddhism, with endless cycles of reincarnation, teaches people to perform religious rituals to gain merit, hopefully earning a better go-around in the next life. Behind Buddhism is a complex world of Hindu gods and venerated spirits. In daily crises and fears, the people of Bangkok turn to the spirit world, superstition, and astrology. Spirit houses stand in front of homes to keep the evil spirits outside. Many people wear amulets thought to contain spiritual powers.

The City Pillar Shrine, thought to be inhabited by the city's guardian spirit, was inspired by the Hindu custom of centrally placing a phallic symbol in Shiva temples. This ruling spirit is perhaps why Bangkok is known as "sin city" and for its night life. The prostitution rings have been pulling village girls and boys away from their homes, exploiting them until they are too old or have contracted AIDS.

PRAYER POINTS

1. The prostitution rings have grown, and the AIDS epidemic has increased. Ask God to completely shut down these financially prosperous but sinful and life-damaging prostitution rings. Pray for the women and young people caught in them.

2. AIDS will have an inevitable impact on leadership in coming generations, even in the church. Pray that the spread of this epidemic can be stopped.

3. Pray that street children may be reached with the gospel and that child slavery will end.

4. Pray for biblical teaching to counter the influence of other religions and cults.

5. The lure of materialism is infecting the church. Pray that a biblical perspective on money and stewardship will come.

Meaning: "no more enemy"

Country: Burma (Myanmar)*

Population: 4,348,000

Living Standards: Much poverty, slum communities outside the city center

Religious Breakdown:
76.0% Buddhist
10.6% Traditional Ethnic
5.6% Christian
3.8% Muslim
4.0% Other

Status of the Church: Mainly Protestant, both registered and unregistered churches

Major Religious Sites: Shwedagon Pagoda, Kaba Aye Pagoda, Innwa Jail, Sule Pagoda

Yangon
(yahn-**gohn**)

City Significance/History

Some five hundred years before Christ, the Mon people established their empire at this location. Having close relations with Indian kings allowed Buddhism to spread quickly among the Mons. It was on the Singuttara Hill where they chose to build the Shwedagon Pagoda. Buddhist tradition tells that five lotus flowers gave rise to five birds, each carrying a yellow robe or wrap. The robes were for five Buddhas that would reach enlightenment and then guide this world to Nirvana. So far, four of the five Buddhas have appeared. When the fifth, called Maitreya, appears, he will bring the new world cycle. Each of the past four Buddhas have left relics (a staff, filter for water, one of the robes, and eight head hairs) all at Shwedagon.

Throughout history, pilgrims have come to this pagoda, bringing their offerings and hoping for Nirvana to come quickly. The high place of the hilltop pagoda made it strategic.

The British, in their quest to control more trade in the East, captured Shwedagon because it overlooked the delta below. The city developed under the British. When the Japanese arrived, they were viewed as liberators from the British rule. Shortly after World War II the country was granted independence. Oppressive and often brutal military regimes have ruled the country since.

PRAYER POINTS

1. Pray for unity between the denominational and evangelical churches.

2. Pray that the church leaders would grow in their vision for the local church, and that the local church would reach out in Jesus' name.

3. Pray for Christian leadership training and other short-term training programs. Pray that more local leaders would move the gospel forward.

4. Pray that the government would change its authoritarian policies.

5. It is very difficult to evangelize Buddhists. Pray that the spiritual strongholds over Buddhism would be broken down.

6. Pray that the physical needs of the poor would be met and that the good news would be preached to them.

India

Bangladesh

DHAKA

91

Meaning: possibly named after a goddess's temple, Dhakeshwari

Country: Bangladesh*

Population: 14,796,000

Living Standards: Over 20% unemployment, many slum areas

Religious Breakdown:
88.0% Muslim
9.6% Hindu
1.4% Christian
1.0% Other

Status of the Church: Roman Catholics and Protestants; slow, steady growth

Major Religious Sites: Hassain Dolan Mosque, Baitul Mukarram Mosque, Kashaitully Mosque, Holy Resurrection Armenian Church

Dhaka
(**dah**-kuh)

City Significance/History

Dhaka was established at its present site in the fourth century because of the agricultural wealth along the Buriganga River. Because of the flooded coastal deltas and the Chittagong Hills, today the majority of the population lives in the central plains.

Few outsiders ventured to this isolated city until the mid-eighteenth century, when the Mongol Empire extended its borders once again, this time including Bengal. Dhaka became a regional capital.

When the British entered the Indian subcontinent, Bengal came under their authority. After independence in 1971, the country went through a civil war and emerged as Bangladesh. The population has continued to explode.

Famines and natural disasters have plagued the country and city, keeping poverty high. Many people from all regions have relocated to Dhaka, hoping for a better life. The old section of Dhaka, called Sadarghat, has been a growing slum that provides few opportunities for the poor to improve their lot. The stagnation of the economy has seen even the educated fall into poverty. Through the now famous Grameen Bank, established in the 1970s and headquartered in Dhaka, the poor can receive loans to establish small businesses.

PRAYER POINTS

1. Pray that the government's increasingly restrictive laws against Christians will be modified, and that Islamist groups will not prevail in restricting other religions.

2. Pray for an increased response to the gospel from Muslims, and that church leaders coming from a Muslim background will have the strength to persevere and to withstand persecution.

3. The Great Commission Movement was launched in 1991 to plant churches and reach ethnic groups. Pray that its goals would be reached and for the church to grow.

4. Pray that Christian media, literature, and Bibles would continue to reap a harvest and that the demand can be met.

5. Pray that the Prince of Peace might be known on university campuses, where gang warfare has taken many lives.

Meaning: "muddy river confluence"

Country: Malaysia*

Population: 1,519,000

Living Standards: High for some; much poverty among rural migrants

Religious Breakdown:
55.0% Muslim
17.0% Buddhist
12.0% Chinese folk-religionist
7.0% Hindu
4.5% Christian
4.5% Other

Status of the Church: Growing Protestant churches, mainly ethnic Chinese and Indian

Major Religious Sites: Jamek Mosque, Negara Mosque, Sri Mahamariamman Temple, International Buddhist Pagoda, Batu Caves

Kuala Lumpur

(**kwah**-luh **loom**-poor)

City Significance/History

Prospecting for tin brought an influx of people in 1857 to where the Mang and Gombak rivers converge. Soon after tin was found, Kuala Lumpur became a boomtown. People came from as far as China to mine tin.

The city never looked back. It has grown to be the capital and largest city of Malaysia—a cultural hub and business center, particularly for the rubber and tin industries. The makeup of Kuala Lumpur includes Chinese, Indian (brought in by the British to work the rubber plantations), and the ethnic Malay.

These three ethnic groups have vastly different religious beliefs (Buddhism, Hinduism, and Islam). Yet in a region most often associated with Buddhism and animism, the Malays stand out as a strong Islamic force. To be Malay is to be Muslim. For a Malay to become a Christian means to leave his or her cultural roots.

The government has closed the doors for Christian outreach to Malays, but there are no restrictions on witnessing to non-Malays. It is illegal for anyone to proselytize the ethnic Malay. For Christians to reach out to Malays means prosecution and possible imprisonment.

PRAYER POINTS

1. Pray against a spirit of superstition among the Malays, who employ the service of the local *bomoh*, "spirit magician," to deal with spiritual issues. Pray that God will continue to reveal himself through dreams and visions.

2. Divorce is common in Malay society because of a lack of trust in many marriages. Pray for the establishment of Christian ministries to answer this problem.

3. Pray that government restrictions against evangelizing the Malays will be lifted and that persecution of Malay converts and believers who witness to them will cease.

4. Pray that household evangelism to Buddhists and Hindus will bear much fruit.

5. Pray for unity in the church despite persecution, and that God would strengthen the pastors and leaders.

Meaning: "place of victory"

Country: Indonesia*

Population: 9,703,000

Living Standards: High for some; much poverty among rural migrants

Religious Breakdown:
72.0% Muslim
21.0% Christian
2.5% Traditional Ethnic
2.0% Hindu
2.5% Other

Status of the Church: One thousand registered churches, thousands of cell churches

Major Religious Sites: Istiqlal Mosque, Al Azhar Mosque, Vihara Dharma Jaya Temple, Wisma Subud Cilandak Headquarters, Gereja Sion Church

Jakarta
(juh-**kahr**-tuh)

City Significance/History

Hindu travelers found the port of Sunda Kelapa in Jakarta useful for protection from storms and a good trade center. Control by the Hindu powers passed to traders from the northern islands who brought Islam. By the sixteenth century, European forces were vying for control of the wealth and trade. The British and Dutch both set up trading posts; however, it was the Dutch who finally established a fort and gained control of the area. It became their hub for administration in all of the East Indies.

At the end of World War II, Jakarta was freed from Japanese domination, and it became the capital of the independent country of Indonesia. The abortive communist coup in 1965 produced much bloodshed. Indonesia became a democracy in 1999.

As the country's population has exploded in the past fifty years, Jakarta has become a modern city with tremendous slums. The arrival of villagers from economically depressed rural areas pushed the slums to over 60 percent of the city's population in the early 1970s. Shantytowns have been hid behind modern buildings, and the government has been relocating many of the poor to other islands.

PRAYER POINTS

1. Pray that the government will promote the development of a pluralistic nation in which all religions have full freedom of worship.

2. More Muslims live in Indonesia than in any other nation. Pray that millions of Muslims will hear and respond to the truth of the gospel.

3. Pray that the process of modernization will not destroy traditional family life.

4. Pray that God will use the press and electronic media as a means to glorify his name — that Christian programming would be abundant.

5. Pray for the continued growth of the church and for mature leaders to lead the new believers in truth.

Meaning: unknown

Country: Brunei*

Population: 82,000

Living Standards: Oil and natural gas have produced wealth

Religious Breakdown:
61.0% Muslim
11.0% Traditional Ethnic
10.0% Buddhist
9.0% Christian
5.0% Chinese Religions
4.0% Other

Status of the Church: A few Chinese fellowships, no known Malay believers

Major Religious Sites: Omar Ali Saifuddin Mosque, Tomb of Sultan Bolkiah

Bandar Seri Begawan

(**buhn**-der **ser**-ee buh-**gah**-wahn)

City Significance/History

Located at the mouth of the Brunei River and protected by the Brunei Bay, Bandar Seri Begawan has been a seat of power for the control of northern Borneo to the Philippines. The city overlooks the bay where European ships would rest and seek trade. But with time the power of the sultan in the area declined, and pirates began to prey on European trade ships as they passed.

Islam entered the country in the fifteenth century through the conversion of Sultan Awang Alak Beter. He was a pagan ruler until he heard about Islam, probably through Muslim traders. To show his desire to be identified with Islam, he changed his name to Sultan Muhammad, after the founder of Islam.

The British had developed strong trade routes between China, India, and England. Piracy was something they could not allow. The British captured the area in the early nineteenth century, making the country a British protectorate until 1984. Oil was found off the coast over fifty years ago, and the wealth of the city again grew.

The current sultan, one of the world's richest men, represents one of the oldest, continuously ruling dynasties in the world. Christians in Brunei are under an increasing amount of pressure as the nation becomes increasingly Islamic.

PRAYER POINTS

1. Currently no Christian literature may be imported. Pray that Christian literature may be imported and that contact with foreign Christians be allowed.

2. Pray that evangelism among the Muslims will be allowed.

3. Pray that the government leaders will provide constitutional protection to Christians and allow for public celebration of Christmas.

4. Pray that God would soften the heart of the current sultan and allow his nation to turn to Christ.

5. Pray for disillusionment with the materialism brought by oil money and that the people would desire true riches in Jesus Christ.

Russia

ULAANBAATAR

Mongolia

China

95

Ulaanbaatar
(oo-lahn-**bah**-tor)

Meaning: "red warrior"

Country: Mongolia*

Population: 919,000

Living Standards: One-quarter of population is considered poor

Religious Breakdown:
36.0% Nonreligious
32.0% Traditional Ethnic
24.0% Buddhist
5.0% Muslim
2.5% Christian
0.5% Other

Status of the Church: Growing number of Christians; various denominations

Major Religious Sites: Gandan Monastery, Mongolian Astrologers Center

City Significance/History

The Gobi Desert and steppes of Mongolia have historically produced warriors who have conquered vast territories. The Great Wall of China was built to keep the Mongols out. (The wall never physically failed; it was the watchtower guards being bribed that allowed the Mongols through.) Central Asia and Persia saw the Mongols sweep through. The great unifier of the Mongols, Genghis Khan ("universal king"), expanded the Mongol Empire to Arabia, Russia, and China.

In the seventeenth century Ulaanbaatar became the home of Jebtsundamba Hutuktu, one of the revelations of the living Buddha. Almost one hundred years later, Gandan Monastery was built in the city as a Buddhist center and temple.

With the fall of the Mongolian Empire, Mongolia became a territory fought over between China and Russia, at times controlled by one or the other power.

Stalin, in the 1930s, shut down the monasteries and imprisoned the monks because they were too powerful. Communism fell apart in Mongolia in 1990, and religion was able to reestablish itself. Today more Mongols live in China's Inner Mongolia Autonomous Region than in Mongolia itself. About 40 percent of Mongolia's population lives in Ulaanbaatar.

PRAYER POINTS

1. Continuing economic difficulties and unemployment make life hard for Mongol families. Pray that the hardships these people are going through would be alleviated.

2. The city council is requiring churches to register and give the name, gender, workplace, and address of all members. Pray that believers can freely meet and worship, and for the raising up of Mongol leaders to guide new fellowships.

3. Disunity among Christians exists over which Mongolian Bible version is preferable. Pray for consensus on this important issue.

4. Some short-term missionaries have been counterproductive in their witness. Pray for wisdom for those working in the city.

5. Pray that cults and other religions would not confuse new Christians and that the false religions would decrease in popularity.

Meaning: "peaceful ocean"

Country: North Korea*

Population: 3,346,000

Living Standards: Poor living conditions, rationing of foodstuffs, and reliance on foreign food aid

Religious Breakdown:
70.0% Nonreligious
13.0% New Religionist
12.0% Traditional Ethnic
3.5% Christian
1.5% Other

Status of the Church: Three "official" churches, numerous house churches, many imprisoned Christians

Major Religious Sites: Tower of the Juche Idea, Mangyongdae Monument (Sung's birthplace)

Pyongyang
(pyong-yang)

City Significance/History

Since the first millennium BC, Pyongyang has been central for powers ruling the Korean peninsula. The Chinese, Japanese, and the Wang Dynasty all tried to control it. Few Western ideas penetrated the area, but Roman Catholicism did. Farmers followed this new religion. Because the farmers were uneducated and poor, the government paid little attention until some Confucian aristocrats converted.

By the nineteenth century Christian missionaries were sailing up the Taedong River to Pyongyang. The Confucian government attacked and sank one ship. The Rev. Robert Thomas escaped by swimming to shore. It is reported that before he was martyred, he presented a Bible to his executioner, who later became a Christian. Many Korean Christians were persecuted and killed.

By 1930 Pyongyang had changed, becoming Asia's capital of Christianity. However, in 1945, before the Japanese surrendered, Stalin placed troops in northern Korea. The Communist regime that emerged was led by Kim Il Sung. Thousands of Christians were martyred during and after the Korean War.

Kim Il Sung died in 1994 and was succeeded by his son, Kim Jong Il. This Marxist nation remains one of the most closed countries to religion in general and to Christianity.

PRAYER POINTS

1. Pray that the government will change its policy and allow religious freedom, true public worship, and the construction of church buildings.

2. Pray that the house churches would be given growth, opportunity, and freedom to develop into mature congregations. Pray for Christian leaders to be raised up.

3. Pray that believers could be contacted and visited by Christians from the outside and that they could travel to international gatherings.

4. Currently the official church is not allowed to cooperate with outsiders in Bible distribution. Pray that Bibles and Christian literature can be produced, especially for school children. Pray that a press to print Bibles can be established.

5. Pray for national reunification between the South and North. South Korean Christians greatly desire to spread their spiritual fervor northward.

Meaning: "dry, big river"
Country: Japan, Hokkaido*
Population: 2,556,000
Living Standards: Very little poverty
Religious Breakdown:
  58.8% Buddhist and Shintoist
  26.5% New Religionist
  13.0% Nonreligious
  1.2% Christian
  0.5% Other
Status of the Church: Over one hundred indigenous churches
Major Religious Sites: Hokkaido Jingu Shrine

Sapporo
(sah-**poor**-oh)

City Significance/History

Sapporo developed as a small Ainu village. The Ainu were a distinct people from the Japanese but would interact with them in trade. The Ainu traded bear meat and salmon for cloth and iron goods.

The Iyomante festival was the climax of the worship of the bear, one of the animal god-spirits they worshiped. The spirits of the animals were central to their lives; Ainu women would raise (including breast feeding) a bear cub in honor to the animal. The fur and meat of the bear was extremely important to life, and each animal received prayers of thanksgiving and requests for the animal's afterlife.

As the Japanese population increased, the islands to the south needed more land. The outnumbered Ainu people were crushed and were forced to move north by the advancing Japanese. The northern island of Hokkaido fell to the Japanese in the mid-nineteenth century, and Sapporo was then established as their territorial capital in 1869.

In the past one hundred years, the city has grown to be the island's cultural, political, and economic center. In 1972 the Winter Olympics were held here. Ainu culture has mostly disappeared, as the two groups have intermarried.

PRAYER POINTS

1. Pray for unity within the churches—that through cooperation evangelistic outreaches would be effective. Pray also for wisdom in planting new churches.

2. Most homes have a *Butsudan* (Buddhist family altar) for the worship of ancestors. Pray that the generational hold of these family altars would be broken.

3. Pray that the spirit of materialism over the city would be overthrown.

4. Hokkaido has the highest rate of divorce in Japan. Pray that family life will be strengthened and families reconciled through Christ.

5. Pray for believers as they continue to evangelize their neighbors and friends.

6. Pray that the animistic beliefs of the Ainu would be broken and that the strained relationships between the native Ainu and the Japanese will be healed.

China　Russia

North Korea

South Korea

TOKYO-YOKOHAMA

Japan ★

98

Meaning: Tokyo – "eastern capital"; Yokohama – "be the beach"

Country: Japan

Population: 36,094,000

Living Standards: High cost of living, little poverty

Religious Breakdown:
57.0% Buddhist and Shintoist
25.3% New Religionist
13.0% Nonreligious
4.2% Christian
0.5% evangelical

Status of the Church: Mix of denominations

Major Religious Sites: Tokyo – Yasukuni and Meiji Shrines, Kwannon and Kaneiji Temples; Yokohama – Asakusa Amanawa Shrines, Great Buddha Statue, Hasedera Temple

Tokyo-Yokohama

(**toh**-kee-oh yoh-koh-**hah**-mah)

City Significance/History

About five hundred years ago, fishers and rice farmers lived in the small village of Edo. Three rivers joined there, but very little took place in this sleepy village. A fort was built in the mid-sixteenth century to protect the military Shogun (Takugawa) capital. The Shogun rule turned Japan's economy from the wealth of the aristocracy into a commercial state. Edo continued to grow and develop until the eighteenth century, when it hit one million people—the largest city of the time.

As Edo grew, foreigners desired greater contact with the city. The Takugawa government did not want the foreigners in Edo, so they allowed the fishing settlement of Yokohama to house the international community. The development of this port city allowed for foreign trade and technology to increase throughout Japan. Industries were built, and the city grew.

Today, Tokyo and Yokohama make up the most populous metropolitan area in the world. The population continues to increase, and more land has been reclaimed from rivers and the ocean. Tokyo is home to the Japanese Parliament and the powerful Ministry of International Trade and Industry.

PRAYER POINTS

1. A spirit of materialism motivates this global economic center. Pray that God will awaken the city and nation to its need for salvation.

2. Pray against the rise and influence of cults like Mormonism, Jehovah's Witness, and the Unification Church, as well as new Buddhist-influenced religious movements.

3. Pray for the salvation of the Imperial family, and that official visits to the Yasokuni Shrine by politicians will be discontinued.

4. Pray for unity and mutual understanding between noncharismatic and charismatic Christians. Suspicion has led to lack of cooperation and spiritual pride.

5. Pray for strong biblical teaching in churches in the city and nation. Pray that, in turn, Japanese believers will boldly engage in personal evangelism.

Meaning: Osaka – "large slope," Kobe – "door of the gods," Kyoto – "capital city"

Country: Japan

Population: 13,141,000

Living Standards: Little poverty

Religious Breakdown:
57.4% Buddhist and Shintoist
25.5% New Religionist
13.0% Nonreligious
3.6% Christian
0.5% Other

Status of the Church: Mix of denominations

Major Religious Sites: Osaka – Shitennoji Temple, Sumiyoshi and Temmangu Shrines; Kobe – Ikuta-jinja Shrine; Kyoto – Daitokuji and Ryoanji Temples, Kibone Shrine

Osaka-Kobe-Kyoto

(oh-**sah**-kah **koh**-bee **kyoh**-toh)

City Significance/History

Shitennoji Temple was built in Osaka back in the sixth century. Tradition states the temple was constructed by Prince Shotoku, who, during the heat of a battle, vowed to build it to the Shitenno (the four gods who protect the cardinal points of the compass). Osaka had grown and become a center for the Isiyama Honganji. This religious and secular organization built a temple fortress at nearby Kyoto that attracted pilgrims.

From 794 to 1869, Kyoto was the capital of Japan, a religious monarchy at the time. The rise of the Shogun power in Edo (Tokyo) saw the area lose importance to the northern capital. Today Kyoto is the national center of culture and Buddhism, where over two thousand temples and shrines exist. The city recently celebrated its twelve hundredth anniversary.

Osaka Bay was large and protected, a great location for trade with the outside world. In 1868 Commodore Perry forced open the port at Kobe, and foreign trade flourished with few restrictions. This freedom caused the port to expand while Osaka's population growth allowed the two cities to unite.

Industry, business, and international trade have caused the three cities to form the Keihanshin Industrial Zone. It is the largest economic region in the world.

PRAYER POINTS

1. As a pilgrimage site, Kyoto draws over one-third of the Japanese people yearly. Pray that these pilgrims would discover the truth of God in Christ.

2. Pray for business missionaries to enter this economic zone and reach wealthy businesspeople who might not ever go to church.

3. Pray against a sense of national pride and superiority that makes people reject a "foreign religion" like Christianity.

4. Pray for empassioned leaders to pioneer new churches and missions.

5. Pray for believers to have a greater awareness of evil spirits and occultism and their spiritual effect in people's lives.

Meaning: Fukuoka – "blessed hill," Kitakyushu – "north nine states"

Country: Japan

Population: 2,816,000

Living Standards: Little poverty
Religious Breakdown:
58.2% Buddhist and Shintoist
26.0% New Religionist
13.0% Nonreligious
2.3% Christian
0.5% Other

Status of the Church: Mix of denominations

Major Religious Sites: Fukuoka – Shofukuji Temple, Kushida Shrine, Munaga Taisha Shrine, Dazaifu Tenmangu Shrine, Aso Mountain; Kitakyushu – Sumiyoshi Shrine

Fukuoko-Kitakyushu

(foo-koo-**oh**-kah kee-tah-**kyoo**-shoo)

City Significance/History

As early as 300 BC, a fort was located at Hakata Bay. This small community traded with Korea and other lands but was not a power in the area.

In the late sixth century, Fukuoko became the primary city for trade with China. Hakata Bay provided great protection from the ocean, and its location just off of Korea made it a natural springboard for trade with China.

The trade routes brought Zen (deep meditative) Buddhism to Japan in the twelfth century. Today the Shofukuji Temple stands as the oldest Zen temple in Japan.

One hundred years later, Mongol invaders twice tried to conquer Japan

through Hakata Bay. The invasions were not successful, more because of violent typhoons than the Japanese superiority in fighting. Japan was saved from the well-trained Mongol forces.

By the twentieth century the city became an industrial and fishing center. It was the largest city on the island of Kyushu, as well as the political center.

In 1963 five cities of Fukuoka province were incorporated to form Kitakyushu. This united city is now the island's most important industrial center. The local government desires to increase foreign trade and to become Japan's gateway to the rest of Asia.

PRAYER POINTS

1. Pray for revival motivated by a spirit of repentance. Pray that joy and enthusiasm might replace the formality in worship services.

2. Pray that seminaries will teach sound biblical theology so that new graduates will be empowered to lead the church into spiritual growth. Pray for encouragement and spiritual strength for the pastors, that they might be refreshed by the Holy Spirit.

3. Pray against the influence of the Mormons, who built a temple in the city in 2000.

4. Pray that the grip of juvenile delinquency upon the area will be broken and that the Christians ministering to these youth can lead them to the Lord.

5. Pray against occultism and false religions, which are especially targeting the youth.

RESOURCES

Books

The 10/40 Window

A Call to Prayer for the Children, Teens, and Young Adults of the 10/40 Window
by Beverly Pegues and Nancy Huff • ISBN 978-1-57658-255-8

Light the Window: Praying through the Nations of the 10/40 Window
edited by Floyd McClung • ISBN 978-7-57658-150-6

The Move of the Holy Spirit in the 10/40 Window
by Luis Bush and Beverly Pegues • ISBN 978-1-57658-151-3

Strongholds of the 10/40 Window
Intercessor's Guide to the World's Least Evangelized Nations
edited by George Otis Jr. • ISBN 978-0-927545-86-0

Prayer

Intercession, Thrilling and Fulfilling
by Joy Dawson • ISBN 978-1-57658-006-6

Missions and Ministry

Asia: A Christian Perspective
by Mary Ann Lind • ISBN 978-0-961553-44-9

Becoming a World Changing Family
Fun & Innovative Ways to Spread the Good News
by Donna S. Thomas • ISBN 978-1-57658-452-1

The Book that Transforms Nations
The Power of the Bible to Change Any Country
by Loren Cunningham • ISBN 978-1-57658-381-4

Discipling Nations: The Power of Truth to Transform Culture
by Darrow L. Miller • ISBN 978-1-57658-248-0

His Kingdom Come: An Integrated Approach to Discipling the Nations
and Fulfilling the Great Commission
edited by Jim Stier, Richlyn Poor, and Lisa Orvis • ISBN 978-1-57658-435-4

Spiritual Warfare for Every Christian
How to Live in Victory and Retake the Land
by Dean Sherman • ISBN 978-0-927545-05-1

Stepping Out: A Guide to Short-Term Missions
ISBN 978-0-927545-29-7

Truth and Transformation: A Manifesto for Ailing Nations
by Vishal Mangalwadi • ISBN 978-1-57658-512-2

Christian Heroes: Then & Now

by Janet and Geoff Benge, for ages 10 and up

Gladys Aylward: The Adventure of a Lifetime • 978-1-57658-019-6
Nate Saint: On a Wing and a Prayer • 978-1-57658-017-2
Hudson Taylor: Deep in the Heart of China • 978-1-57658-016-5
Amy Carmichael: Rescuer of Precious Gems • 978-1-57658-018-9
Eric Liddell: Something Greater Than Gold • 978-1-57658-137-7
Corrie ten Boom: Keeper of the Angels' Den • 978-1-57658-136-0
William Carey: Obliged to Go • 978-1-57658-147-6
George Müller: The Guardian of Bristol's Orphans • 978-1-57658-145-2

Jim Elliot: One Great Purpose • 978-1-57658-146-9
Mary Slessor: Forward into Calabar • 978-1-57658-148-3
David Livingstone: Africa's Trailblazer • 978-1-57658-153-7
Betty Greene: Wings to Serve • 978-1-57658-152-0
Adoniram Judson: Bound for Burma • 978-1-57658-161-2
Cameron Townsend: Good News in Every Language • 978-1-57658-164-3
Jonathan Goforth: An Open Door in China • 978-1-57658-174-2
Lottie Moon: Giving Her All for China • 978-1-57658-188-9
John Williams: Messenger of Peace • 978-1-57658-256-5
William Booth: Soup, Soap, and Salvation • 978-1-57658-258-9
Rowland Bingham: Into Africa's Interior • 978-1-57658-282-4
Ida Scudder: Healing Bodies, Touching Hearts • 978-1-57658-285-5
Wilfred Grenfell: Fisher of Men • 978-1-57658-292-3
Lillian Trasher: The Greatest Wonder in Egypt • 978-1-57658-305-0
Loren Cunningham: Into All the World • 978-1-57658-199-5
Florence Young: Mission Accomplished • 978-1-57658-313-5
Sundar Singh: Footprints Over the Mountains • 978-1-57658-318-0
C.T. Studd: No Retreat • 978-1-57658-288-6
Rachel Saint: A Star in the Jungle • 978-1-57658-337-1
Brother Andrew: God's Secret Agent • 978-1-57658-355-5
Clarence Jones: Mr. Radio • 978-1-57658-343-2
Count Zinzendorf: Firstfruit • 978-1-57658-262-6
John Wesley: The World His Parish • 978-1-57658-382-1
C. S. Lewis: Master Storyteller • 978-1-57658-385-2
David Bussau: Facing the World Head-on • 978-1-57658-415-6
Jacob DeShazer: Forgive Your Enemies • 978-1-57658-475-0
Isobel Kuhn: On the Roof of the World • 978-1-57658-497-2
Paul Brand: Helping Hands • 978-1-57658-536-8
D. L. Moody: Bringing Souls to Christ • 978-1-57658-552-8
Dietrich Bonhoeffer: In the Midst of Wickedness • 978-1-57658-713-3

Websites

Joshua Project, www.joshuaproject.net
Window International Network, www.win1040.com
The 30-Days Prayer Network, www.30-days.net